A CELEBRA...

DOL... PARTON

ACTIVITY BOOK

Nathan Joyce

Illustrations by Juhee Kim

PORTICO

First published in the United Kingdom in 2021 by
Portico
43 Great Ormond Street
London
WC1N 3HZ

An imprint of Pavilion Books Company Ltd

Illustrations by Juhee Kim

ISBN 978-1-911622-70-3

A CIP catalogue record for this book is available from the British Library.

10 9 8 7 6 5 4 3 2 1

Reproduction by Mission Productions Ltd, Hong Kong
Printed and bound by Imak Ofset, Turkey

www.pavilionbooks.com

Publisher: Helen Lewis
Editor: Izzy Holton
Design Manager: Alice Kennedy-Owen
Production Controller: Phil Brown

CONTENTS

★ ★

Introduction

I've been lucky enough to write books about my three favourite people in the past couple of years: David Attenborough, Michelle Obama and now Dolly Parton! I've just got Martin Luther King and J.R.R. Tolkien to go, and I've worked my way through my entire dream dinner party set!

Dolly Parton is a ray of sunshine. And there's no one who doesn't like sunshine. In November 2019, despairing at the political situation in the US, *The New York Times* published an article with the heading:

'Is There Anything We Can All Agree On?
Yes: Dolly Parton'

Damn straight.

Donating $1 million to Vanderbilt University Medical Center in April 2020, and finding out on live TV at the same time as everyone else that your money actually helped create a vaccine for COVID-19? Amazing. And then singing a parody version of 'Jolene' before you get the jab, singing, 'Vaccine, vaccine, vaccine, vacccciiine'? Off the scale.

So what is it about Dolly? Well, to start with, it's a rags-to-riches story – and we're talking real rags, too, growing up with 11 siblings in a one-room cabin that got so cold in winter that water would freeze *inside* the house. So poor that her daddy paid the doctor who delivered Dolly with a sack of cornmeal.

Dolly followed her dreams with passion and grit, and didn't take no for an answer. But she also mastered the art of not getting pushed around, famously scolding tough guy Sylvester Stallone while they filmed *Rhinestone* for the way he treated a homeless guy. And she had the courage to say no to Elvis's manager when he demanded too much from Dolly to cover 'I Will Always Love You', and the wisdom to say yes when the right deal came up in the shape of Whitney Houston's unforgettable version of 1992.

Dolly cares about people and she's proud of who she is and where she came from. She's a real person, and that vulnerability and honesty comes across in her lyrics. And then there's the small matter of having a voice like a nightingale and being a songwriting phenomenon.

She champions people who have struggled, and not because it's fashionable to do so or it might help her financially. She wants to help. And she'll be there on the front lines, whether it's raising money to help victims of the 2016 Great Smoky Mountain wildfires or pioneering her Imagination Library, the free book-gifting programme that has benefited children all over the world.

She's also wonderfully mischievous, completely outrageous and will make interviewers fall off their chairs with laughter with one of her turns of phrase (which have become known as Dollyisms). Everyone knows one of them, from the disarming, 'It costs a lot of money to look this cheap' to the philosophical, 'The way I see it, if you want the rainbow, you gotta put up with the rain' to the hilarious, 'It's a good thing I was born a girl, otherwise I'd be a drag queen!'

For all these reasons and a thousand more, we love you, Dolly. I'm just praying that she comes to my home town of Brighton and plays Pride one year. Please, Dolly!

Dolly True or False?

1 Dolly's father paid for the birth of Dolly with a sack of cornmeal

2 Dolly has never been on any of the rides at Dollywood because she's afraid of rollercoasters

3 Dolly was originally cast to play Sugar 'Kane' Kowalczyk in *Some Like It Hot* before the role went to Marilyn Monroe

4 Dolly received death threats from KKK members after Dollywood joined other amusement parks in celebrating 'Gay Days' at the park in support of the LGBTQ+ community

5 'Jolene' was inspired by a real person

6 Dolly met her husband-to-be outside a laundromat

7 The British confectionery 'Dolly mixture' is named after Dolly

8 Dolly once entered a Dolly Parton lookalike contest ... and lost

9 Dolly sleeps in her make-up

10 Dolly's style icon growing up was the town tramp

Some of the things that have happened to Dolly along the way are beyond belief, aren't they? Before we dive in, test yourself and see if you can find the four lies! (Answers on page 187)

11 A fan once left a baby in a box on Dolly's porch

16 Dolly credits her dog Popeye with saving her life after having her heart broken

12 Dolly can occasionally be spotted at a Taco Bell drive thru with her husband Carl

17 Dolly saved the life of a child actor on the set of *Christmas on the Square* in 2020

13 Dolly was made an honorary Dame by Queen Elizabeth II in 2001

18 Dolly tried to buy Disneyland Paris in 1993 after a disappointing opening year for the park

14 Dolly turned down the Presidential Medal of Freedom twice from the Trump administration

19 Dolly once won a Rodeo competition in Montana in 1977

15 Dolly is Miley Cyrus's godmother

20 You can hear the sound of Dolly's acrylic nails tapping in '9 to 5'

Dolly's Greatest Hits

Here are Dolly's albums and singles that have been certified as gold and platinum by the Recording Industry Association of America and the year they earned that certification. Why not find yourself a gold pen (and for platinum, go with silver mixed with a bit of grey) and colour in the discs!

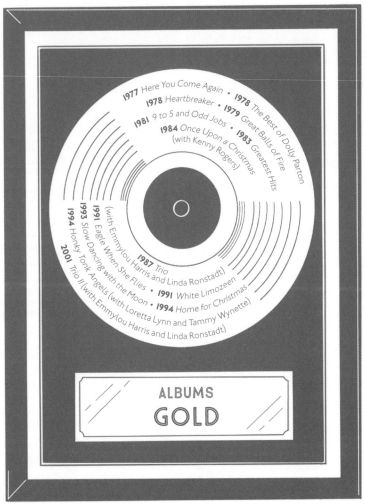

1977 Here You Come Again • **1978** The Best of Dolly Parton
1978 Heartbreaker • **1979** Great Balls of Fire
1981 9 to 5 and Odd Jobs • **1983** Greatest Hits
1984 Once Upon a Christmas (with Kenny Rogers)
1987 Trio (with Emmylou Harris and Linda Ronstadt)
1991 Eagle When She Flies
1993 Slow Dancing with the Moon • **1991** White Limozeen
1994 Honky Tonk Angels (with Loretta Lynn and Tammy Wynette)
1994 Home for Christmas
2001 Trio II (with Emmylou Harris and Linda Ronstadt)

ALBUMS
GOLD

1978 _Here You Come Again_
1984 _Once Upon a Christmas_ (with Kenny Rogers)
1986 _Greatest Hits_
1987 _Trio_ (with Emmylou Harris and Linda Ronstadt)
1992 _Eagle When She Flies_
1993 _Slow Dancing with the Moon_

ALBUMS
PLATINUM

1989 _Once Upon a Christmas_ (with Kenny Rogers)

ALBUMS
DOUBLE-PLATINUM

1978 'Here You Come Again'
1981 '9 to 5'
1983 'Islands in the Stream' (with Kenny Rogers)
2015 'When I Get Where I'm Going' (with Brad Paisley)
2017 'I Will Always Love You'
2017 'Jolene'

SINGLES
GOLD

1983 'Islands in the Stream' (with Kenny Rogers)
2016 'When I Get Where I'm Going' (with Brad Paisley) • **2017** '9 to 5'

SINGLES
PLATINUM

WALK OF FAME STAR

Here's your chance to decorate
Dolly's Walk of Fame Star as the Smoky Mountain
Songbird would like it – it's far too plain as it is! She received
her first star in 1984, located at 6712 Hollywood Boulevard, and
a joint star, with Emmylou Harris and Linda Ronstadt, in 2018,
in recognition of their work as a trio.

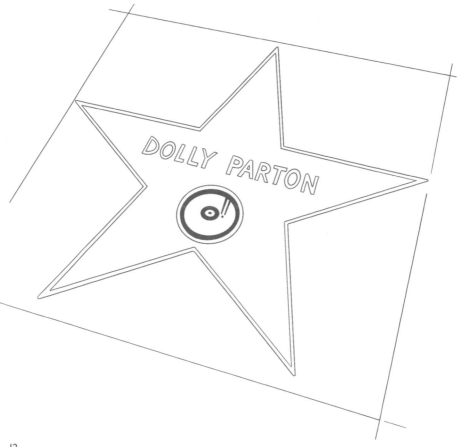

'THE WAY I SEE IT, IF YOU WANT THE RAINBOW, YOU GOTTA PUT UP WITH THE RAIN.'

WIT & WISDOM
'Dollyisms'

Dolly is renowned for her quick-witted quips, known affectionately as 'Dollyisms', some of which have become legendary. Here are some of her funniest.

'It takes a lot of time and money to look this cheap, honey!'

DOLLY: MY LIFE AND OTHER UNFINISHED BUSINESS

'The only way I'd be caught without make-up is if my radio fell in the bathtub while I was taking a bath and electrocuted me and I was in between make-up at home. I hope my husband would slap a little lipstick on me before he took me to the morgue.'

INTERVIEW WITH OPRAH WINFREY

'I tried every diet in the book. I tried some that weren't in the book. I tried eating the book. It tasted better than most of the diets.'

DOLLY: MY LIFE AND OTHER UNFINISHED BUSINESS

'I describe my look as a blend of Mother Goose, Cinderella, and the local hooker!'

DREAM MORE: CELEBRATE THE DREAMER IN YOU

'I'm comfortable in my own skin, no matter how far it's stretched.'

INTERVIEW WITH *THE TIMES*

'I look just like the girl next door... if you happen to live next door to an amusement park.'

HARPER'S BAZAAR ARTICLE

'I like to buy clothes that are two sizes too small and then take them in a little.'

DREAM MORE: CELEBRATE THE DREAMER IN YOU

'If there's a heaven, I hope to hell I go!'

TWITTER POST FROM MARCH 2015

'I'm not offended by dumb-blonde jokes because I know that I'm not dumb. I also know I'm not blonde.'

TWITTER POST FROM JANUARY 2016

'If I have one more facelift, I'll have a beard!'

INTERVIEW WITH *BUST* MAGAZINE

'I have little feet because nothing grows in the shade.'

TWITTER POST FROM FEBRUARY 2011

'I got songs stuck everywhere. I pull out a drawer to get some panties. I'll find a song in there.'

INTERVIEW WITH JOURNALIST DAN RATHER ABOUT SONGWRITING

'If something is bagging, sagging or dragging, I'll tuck it, suck it or pluck it.'

INTERVIEW WITH *THE GUARDIAN*

'The way I look was really a country girl's idea of what glamour was. I patterned my look after the town tramp. I thought she was the prettiest thing in the world, with all that bleached hair and bright-red lipstick. People would say, 'Oh, she's just trash,' and I'd think, 'That's what I want to be when I grow up.'

INTERVIEW WITH *ROLLING STONE*

DOLLY'S GRAMMY WINS

The Grammys recognize achievements in the music industry and are considered one of the 'big four' entertainment awards in the US along with the Emmy Awards for television, the Tony Awards for theatre and the Academy Awards for film. The first Grammy Awards were held in 1959 at the Beverly Hills Hilton, with Ella Fitzgerald picking up two awards, for Best Individual Jazz Performance and Best Pop Vocal Performance. Dolly has picked up 50 nominations and won 11 of the gilded gramophone trophies.

Year	Award	Work
1978	Best Country Vocal Performance, Female	*Here You Come Again*
1981	Best Country Vocal Performance, Female	'9 to 5'
1981	Best Country Song	'9 to 5'
1987	Best Country Performance by a Duo or Group with Vocal	*Trio* (with Emmylou Harris and Linda Ronstadt)
1999	Best Country Collaboration with Vocals	'After the Gold Rush' (with Emmylou Harris and Linda Ronstadt)
2000	Best Bluegrass Album	*The Grass is Blue*
2001	Best Female Country Vocal Performance	*Shine*
2011	Grammy Lifetime Achievement Award	–
2016	Best Country Duo/Group Performance	'Jolene' (with Pentatonix)
2019	Best Contemporary Christian Music Performance/Song	'God Only Knows' (with For King & Country)
2020	Best Contemporary Christian Music Performance/Song	'There Was Jesus'

N.B. The dates on this page reflect the year the records were released and not the year that the Grammy was presented, which is always the year after.

DECORATE YOUR DOLLY BUTTERFLY

Butterflies are Dolly's favourite creature. The 'w' in her Dollywood logo is a butterfly. She has several butterfly tattoos and apparently the bottom of her swimming pool even features a butterfly!

As she says herself:

'Butterflies are my symbol. As a child, I used to get lost chasing them and got my butt whipped for wandering too far off. So we have butterflies everywhere.'

Dolly the Philanthropist

COVID-19 RESEARCH

In April 2020, a month after the World Health Organization declared that COVID-19 had become a pandemic, Dolly donated $1 million (£800,000) towards research efforts at the Vanderbilt University Medical Center in Tennessee. She did this in honour of her friend, Dr Naji N. Abumrad, a surgical professor at the university whom Dolly had met after she was treated at Vanderbilt after being involved in a car accident in 2013. Dr Abumrad had told her that they were making some 'exciting advancements' in the search for a vaccine.

It turns out that Dolly's donation helped to fund Moderna's COVID-19 vaccine – which was granted approval for use in the US on 18 December 2020.

Dolly only found out exactly what her donation had helped to achieve minutes before she appeared on NBC's *Today* programme on 17 November. The producers had learned that Dolly's name appeared among the sponsors in *The New England Journal of Medicine* report on the Moderna vaccine trial.

Dr Abumrad said, 'Her work made it possible to expedite the science behind the testing,' before adding: 'Without a doubt in my mind, her funding made the research toward the vaccine go ten times faster than it would be without it.'

Dolly said, 'I felt like this was the time for me to open my heart and my hand, and try to help.'

Is it possible to love Dolly more?

Coat of Many Colours

Dolly rocks the glitz and glamour. But don't be caught mentioning the word 'fashion' around her. She famously said, 'I would never stoop so low as to be fashionable, that's the easiest thing in the world to do.'

She wore this coat-dress to the premiere of *Coat of Many Colors*, a 2015 TV movie based on Dolly's early life. The title was taken from the song Dolly wrote in 1971 about the patchwork coat Dolly's mother made her out of rags when she was a young child. To make her daughter believe it was special, she told Dolly the biblical story of Joseph and his coat of many colours. When Dolly went to school, thinking she looked like Joseph, children laughed at her for having a coat made of rags. She wrote the song to teach people about bullying, acceptance and the value of kind parents who were rich in love.

Here's your chance to colour it in in your favourite colours!

WORD CLOUD

UNIVERSITY OF TENNESSEE COMMENCEMENT ADDRESS

In 2009, Dolly was invited to give the commencement address to the graduating students of the University of Tennessee. It was a memorable speech full of inspiration and encouragement and went viral on YouTube. Here are the words that cropped up the most in Dolly's speech: the bigger the word appears, the more frequently Dolly used it.

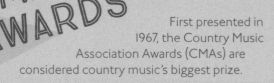

CMA AWARDS

First presented in 1967, the Country Music Association Awards (CMAs) are considered country music's biggest prize.

Here are the CMAs that Dolly's picked up over the years. She suffered a little bit of a wardrobe malfunction in 1978 just before Johnny Cash read out her name. Oh no! But Dolly didn't panic. First, she grabbed an (emergency) big fur stole belonging to Kenny Rogers' wife and walked out on stage. To much laughter from both the crowd and herself, she said:

'I had this dress made in case I won and about five minutes ago, I was hoping I wouldn't win because I busted the front out of it!'

1968	Vocal Group of the Year	Dolly Parton and Porter Wagoner
1970	Vocal Duo of the Year	Dolly Parton and Porter Wagoner
1971	Vocal Duo of the Year	Dolly Parton and Porter Wagoner
1975	Female Vocalist of the Year	–
1976	Female Vocalist of the Year	–
1978	Entertainer of the Year	–
1988	Vocal Event of the Year	*Trio* (with Emmylou Harris and Linda Ronstadt)
1996	Vocal Event of the Year	'I Will Always Love You' (with Vince Gill)
2006	Musical Event of the Year	'When I Get Where I'm Going' (with Brad Paisley)
2016	Willie Nelson Lifetime Achievement Award	–

DECORATE DOLLY'S GUITAR

Dolly's first guitar was given to her by her uncle Lewis when she was a girl. She said:

'He had this little Martin guitar that I loved, so when he saw how serious I was about my music, he gave me his little Martin guitar. It was my treasure.'

When Dolly left home at 18, though, she put it in the loft, wishing that one day she'd be rich enough to fix it up. But, sadly, it was badly damaged in a house fire and only the neck of it remains.

But, don't worry, all is not lost! Here's your chance to design a guitar and case that you know she'd love.

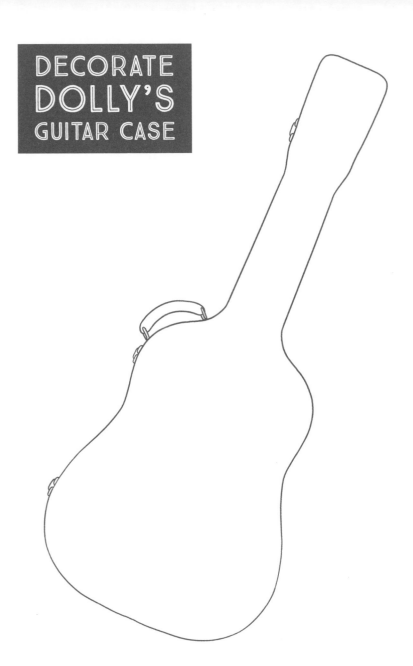

DECORATE
DOLLY'S
GUITAR CASE

DOLLYWOOD

'I was looking up at the big sign that says Hollywood, and I thought,
"Wouldn't it be great if someday I could jerk that big ol' H down
and put a D there to make it Dollywood?" 11 years ago I got
to see that dream come true in the mountains.'

Dollywood is the name of the amusement park that Dolly has famously
co-owned since 1986. It was formerly Silver Dollar City Tennessee,
but changed its name after Dolly bought a stake in it. On the day of
its re-opening as 'Dollywood', the queue of cars trying to enter the
amusement park stretched back for six miles!

In the first year after re-opening, park attendance doubled to a million
annual visitors. Among its attractions are Lightning Rod, the world's
fastest wooden rollercoaster (reaching speeds of 73mph); there's also
the Chasing Rainbows Museum, which tells Dolly's life story, and the
Eagle Mountain Sanctuary, a 30,000-square-foot aviary for injured
eagles. Apparently, Dolly used to have a secret apartment above
Apple Jack's sandwich restaurant.

In 2010, Dollywood won the Liseberg Applause Award,
considered the Oscar of the amusement park industry.
That year, Dolly said of Dollywood:

'I always thought that if I made it big or got successful at what I had started
out to do, that I wanted to come back to my part of the country and do
something great, something that would bring a lot of jobs into this area'.

Sadly though, Dolly's never ridden any of the rides in her own park.
The reason?

'I'm afraid I will lose my hair, my shoes, my boobs may jump out,'
she says!

WHERE'S DOLLY?

Can you spot the super-mini Dolly here at Dollywood? (Answer on page 187)

Rags to Riches

'If it hadn't been for music, I'd have been a beautician ... Even if I wasn't in show business, I would have wanted all the glamour – and that's about the only way a girl in a small Southern town is going to get it, being a beautician.'

SATURDAY EVENING POST, 1989

'Our house had running water, if you were willing to run and get it.'

STYLIST MAGAZINE INTERVIEW

'I've always kinda been a little outcast myself, a little oddball, doin' my thing, my own way. And it's been hard for me too, to be accepted, certainly in the early years of my life.'

'I grew up poor, so poor my daddy paid the doctor who delivered me with a sack of cornmeal.'

GUIDEPOSTS MAGAZINE INTERVIEW

'My songs are the door to every dream I've ever had and every success I've ever achieved.'

'I just love what I do. I never outgrew my childhood and my family and my people ... that keeps me anchored, that keeps me grounded. I'm just doing what I've always wanted to do, what I dreamed of doing, so it makes me happy.'

ACCESS HOLLYWOOD INTERVIEW, 2010

'I had a gift of rhyme and a big imagination and that's just how I started ... and how I'm still a–goin'.'

LOS ANGELES TIMES INTERVIEW, 2019

'Never ignore your roots, your home or your hair.'

'I've said that I had to get rich in order to sing like I was poor again. But I count my blessings more than I count my money.'

HOT PRESS MAGAZINE INTERVIEW

'I'm just a working girl. I never think of myself as a star because somebody once said, "A star is nothing but a big ball of gas" – and I don't want to be that.'

BILLBOARD INTERVIEW, 2014

DESIGN YOUR OWN DOLLYWOOD DODGEM

Terrific news – Dollywood is building a new dodgem arena, and you've been asked to design one of the cars!

1946 QUIZ

Dolly shares the year of her birth with some amazing folks.
Can you guess who they are from the clues? (Answers on page 187)

1 Born Farrokh Bulsara, this chap fronted a regal–sounding rock band

2 President often known by a single letter

3 From *Rocky* to *Rhinestone* alongside Dolly in 1984

4 Iconic singer and actor – the only artist to have a number 1 in each of the past six decades

5 Known for his villainous acting turns including Hans Gruber and the Sheriff of Nottingham

6 The man in the director's chair for *Jurassic Park* and *Jaws*

7 'Let's Stay Together' singer and reverend

8 *Cabaret* queen and daughter of Judy Garland

9 Italian fashion designer and brother of Donatella

10 The 'Louise' to Geena Davis's 'Thelma'

AN UNUSUAL HONOUR

Dolly's won many awards and accolades during her career, but having a fossilized moss and a newly discovered species of fungus named after you must surely top everything else. Right?

In 2015, a previously undiscovered fungus – well, a lichen if we're being technical – was found growing in the Unicoi Mountains near the border between Tennessee and North Carolina. The scientists who made the discovery – Jessica L. Allen and James C. Lendemer – named it *Japewiella dollypartoniana* in Dolly's honour.

Here's how Jessica and James described their discovery:

'As we sat on that rocky summit, we could not help but think of the inspiring example of Dolly Parton. Ms Parton grew up in a small cabin on the edge of the Smokies in Tennessee, rising from humble roots to stardom. Just as we have climbed the great peaks of the southern mountains to document new and endangered lichens, she has climbed to the top of the music charts and met with success. During her lifelong journey, Ms Parton has strived to bring attention to, and support, her native region.'

And then, in 2020, a 460-million-year-old moss, which may have been one of the first plants to grow on land, was discovered by University of Oregon geologist Greg Retallack. The rocks containing the fossils were found only a stone's throw (well, if you could throw five miles) from Dollywood. The name of the new moss? *Dollyphyton boucotil*. Amazing.

SONG ANAGRAMS

Can you guess the Dolly hits lurking
among the letters below? (Answers on page 187)

1. EEL JON _____

2. AWAY ILLUSIVE WOOLLY _____

3. DISMANTLES HAIRNETS _____

4. ABSEIL IVORY KETTLEFUL _____

5. JACKAL PEP _____

6. YES SO WE ROLL _____

7. CARTOON FOOLS YMCA _____

8. REHAB RETAKER _____

9. SWIRLED WOLF _____

10. FINITE OVEN _____

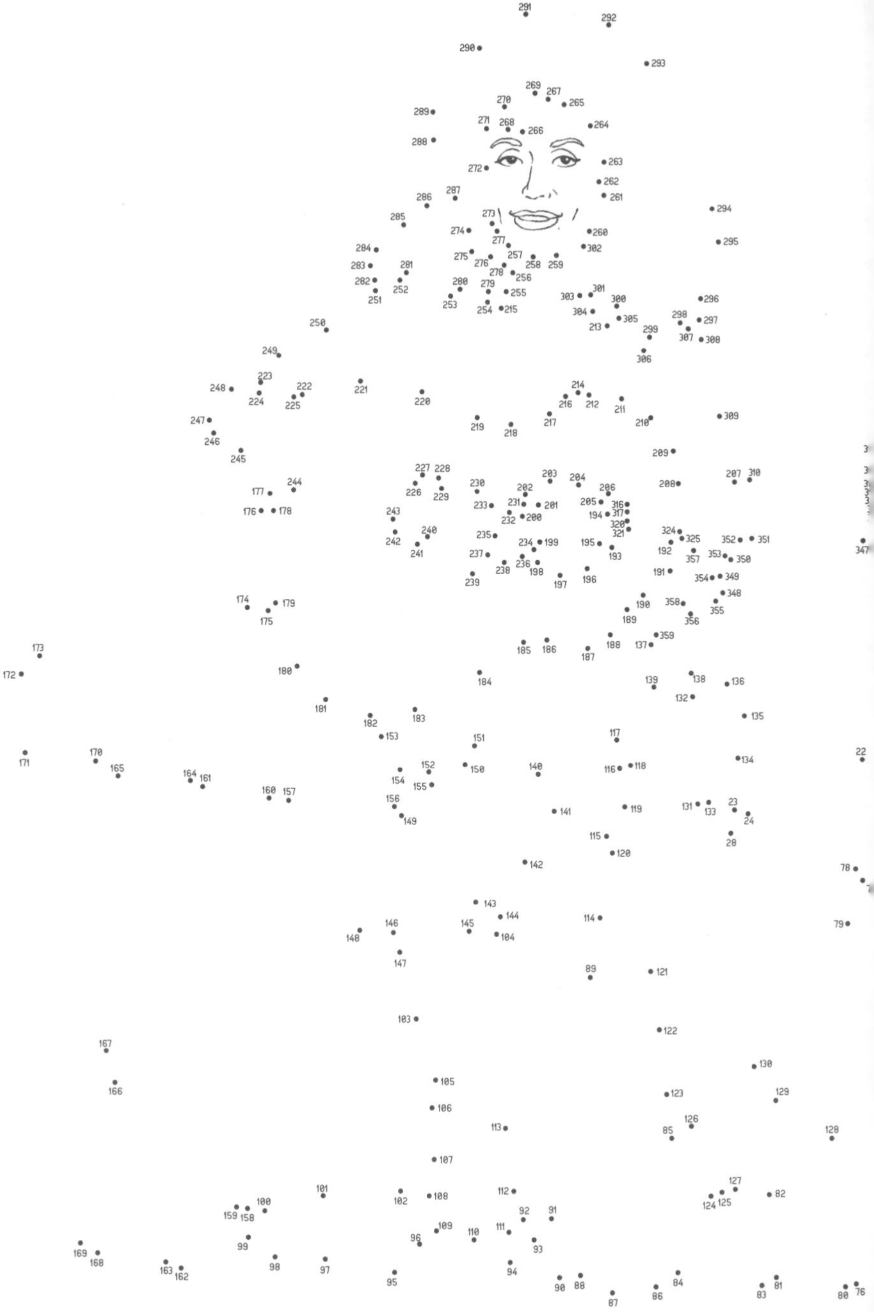

Dolly Dot-to-dot

Join the dots to find Dolly doing what she does best!

4
335
332
334
5
29
333
341
331 342
344 343 340
45

336
337
338
339

361
360
362
20
19
363
365
366
21
25
26
15
364
367
27
14 13
12
11 7
6
18

17
16
30 31
74
73 72
32
33
64
35
34
59
58
9
36
37
57
52
51
10
8
44
43 39
4
38
3
1 2
63
56
50

START

END ▼
368
5

65
69 68
47
66
42
40
62 60
61
55 53
54
49 48 46 45
41
71 70 67
75

33

SPOT THE DOLLY DIFFERENCE

Can you spot the seven differences between this illustration of Dolly and the one opposite? (Answers on page 187)

'FIND THE GUITAR' MAZE

Dolly's about to go on stage but, as luck would have it, someone's hidden her favourite guitar at the end of a maze! (I blame Willie Nelson.) Can you rescue it for her?

(Answer on page 187)

ADVICE TO HER YOUNGER SELF

Dolly revealed the advice she would share with her younger self in an interview with *USA Today* in August 2020 when she was named one of their Women of the Century.

DATE :

'I would just say buckle up, you little barefooted hick, and know that you're in for the ride of your life.
This is what you want and you're going to get it, but you're going to have to work for it and try to love it.
Just try to be strong, try to be tough and use all that redneck strength and knowledge you have and connect that with all the good things you can learn from it, but just know that you're a tough little cookie.
You're going to have a wild ride, but you're going to love it.'

DOLLY TIMELINE

1946 Dolly is born in Locust Ridge, Tennessee, on 19 January

1951 Dolly writes her first song – 'Little Tiny Tasseltop', aged six

1956 Dolly gets her first gig as a regular performer on The Cas Walker Farm and Home Hour in Tennessee

1959 Dolly records her first single, 'Puppy Love'

1959 Dolly performs at the Grand Ole Opry for the first time, aged 13, introduced by one Johnny Cash

1962 Dolly and her uncle are signed to Tree Publishing and Mercury Records in Nashville

1966, March Dolly wins her first major award – BMI Song of the Year – for the song 'Put It Off Until Tomorrow', which she wrote with her uncle Bill

1966, May Dolly and Carl Dean marry in Ringgold, Georgia

1967, January Dolly releases two singles which make the Billboard Country Chart, 'Dumb Blonde' (No. 24) and 'Something Fishy' (No. 17)

1967, September Dolly appears on *The Porter Wagoner Show*

1968, January Dolly and Porter release their first album together, *Just Between You and Me*, which peaked at No. 8 on the Billboard Country Albums Chart

1968, October Dolly and Porter win Best Vocal Group of the Year at the CMA Awards

1971 Dolly scores her first No. 1 hit on the Billboard Country Chart with the single 'Joshua'

1974, February The single 'Jolene' reaches No. 1 on the Billboard Country Chart

1974, June The single 'I Will Always Love You' reaches No. 1 on the Billboard Country Chart

1978 Dolly wins her first Grammy in the Best Country Performance, Female, category for the *Here You Come Again* album

1980 Dolly stars in *9 to 5*, her first film, featuring the eponymous hit song, which goes on to reach No. 1 on the Billboard Hot 100 Chart

1982 The single '9 to 5' wins Best Country Song and Best Country Performance, Female, at the Grammys

1984 Dolly is awarded a star on the Hollywood Walk of Fame

1986, May Dollywood opens!

1986, October Dolly is inducted into the Nashville Songwriters Hall of Fame

1987 *Trio*, the first collaborative album by Dolly, Linda Ronstadt and Emmylou Harris, is released, topping the Country Album Chart and reaching No. 6 on the Billboard Chart

1992 Dolly's song 'I Will Always Love You' is released by Whitney Houston, setting a record of 14 weeks at No. 1

1994 Dolly releases her autobiography, *Dolly: My Life and Other Unfinished Business*

1999, September Dolly is inducted into the Country Music Hall of Fame

1999, October Dolly releases her first bluegrass album, *The Grass is Blue*

2001, February *The Grass is Blue* wins a Grammy for Best Bluegrass Album

2001, June Dolly is inducted into the National Academy of Popular Music's Songwriters Hall of Fame

2004 Dolly receives the Living Legend Medal from the Library of Congress

2006 Dolly is awarded the Kennedy Center Honors for her contribution to American culture

2011 Dolly is presented with the Grammy Lifetime Achievement Award by the Recording Academy

2014 Dolly plays the Pyramid Stage at Glastonbury

2018 Dolly is awarded with two Guinness World Records: most hits on the US Hot Country Songs Chart by a female artist and the most decades with a Top 20 hit on Billboard's Hot Country Songs Chart

DOLLY BIOGRAPHY

Early Years

- Dolly Rebecca Parton was born to Avie Lee Caroline Parton (née Owens) and Robert Lee Parton Sr (known as Lee) in Pittman Center, Sevier County, Tennessee, as the snow fell on 19 January 1946. As Avie Lee was having trouble giving birth, Lee rode out to fetch Dr Robert F. Thomas, a missionary and physician who cared for the poor folks in the Great Smoky Mountains. Lee could only offer Dr Thomas a sack of cornmeal by means of payment.

- Lee was an illiterate tobacco farmer and labourer, while Dolly's mother Avie Lee had her work cut out raising 12 children. They all shared a one-room cabin on the bank of the Little Pigeon River, on the edge of the Great Smoky Mountains. There was no running water, indoor plumbing, electricity or telephone.

- The winters were perishingly cold, and there was no guarantee that the whole family would make it through each year. Buckets of water would freeze even inside their house and the snow would come in through the cracks in the walls.

- Dolly grew up hearing her mother singing English, Irish and Welsh folk songs in a 'haunting voice'. Dolly wrote her first song, 'Little Tiny Tasseltop', an ode to a doll made from a cob of corn, aged just six. She was encouraged by her mother, who wrote down the lyrics because Dolly couldn't write yet.

- The whole family would sit out on the porch and play music, often with homemade instruments. Her uncle Bill was so thrilled that Dolly loved music that he gave her a real guitar when she was eight.

- In 1956, aged ten, Dolly got her first break playing the Cas Walker Show in Knoxville with her uncle Bill and it was a big hit. After the gig, she walked up to Cas Walker and said, 'I want to work for you.' Impressed, he took her on for the sum of $5 a show.

- The year Dolly turned thirteen was a huge one for her career. Her uncle Henry Owens secured her a recording session in Louisiana, which led to her first commercial single, 'Puppy Love', released on 20 April 1959.

- Later that year, Uncle Bill landed Dolly a guest appearance on the biggest stage in country music: the Grand Ole Opry in Nashville, Tennessee. He persuaded Opry star Jimmy C. Newman to give up one of his spots. Dolly was introduced to the stage by 27-year-old country star Johnny Cash. She said years later: 'I thought he was the sexiest thing that ever was.'

FAMOUS TENNESSEANS QUIZ

Can you name the following famous folks either born in or resident in the Volunteer State from the clues below? (Answers on page 187)

1 Actor that played Shawshank Prison's contraband smuggler

3 This great lady is 'Simply the Best'

2 Started his directorial career with *Reservoir Dogs* in 1992

4 Multi–award–winning actor, winning an Oscar in *Misery* and also starring as Molly Brown in *Titanic*

5 She's worthy of 'Respect'

6 Pop star who met his first love while working on *The Mickey Mouse Club*

7 American folk hero famous for his raccoon cap

8 What a jackass

9 Hannah Montana; Dolly's goddaughter

10 Soul legend who lent his voice to play *South Park*'s Chef

11 A world-famous whiskey distiller

12 *Legally Blonde* actor and friend of Dolly who loves the state so much that she named her third child Tennessee!

13 Oscar-winning actor who made her Hollywood debut in *Days of Thunder*, alongside her then-boyfriend

14 Country and pop superstar who knows trouble when it walks in

15 Singer-songwriter who won the first season of *American Idol*

DOLLY WORD SEARCH

See if you can find the following 10 words associated with Dolly in the wordsearch below

(Answers on page 188)

COUNTRY	BUTTERFLY
NASHVILLE	HEARTSTRINGS
TENNESSEE	OPRY
SMOKIES	PORTER
DOLLYWOOD	CARL

J	B	V	S	I	Q	C	E	K	L	A	I	X	I
E	U	R	N	A	S	H	V	I	L	L	E	O	J
H	T	Y	X	Z	P	A	C	U	B	L	G	V	K
E	T	S	Z	S	M	O	K	I	E	S	F	E	T
A	E	F	X	A	I	R	R	O	P	R	Y	E	E
R	R	Q	Y	R	D	Y	K	T	P	Y	K	X	N
T	F	S	U	Z	C	O	N	B	E	G	V	Y	N
S	L	P	R	E	G	C	L	Y	Y	R	S	C	E
T	Y	Z	K	V	K	O	S	L	V	F	T	H	S
R	J	Y	B	A	H	U	S	C	Y	B	J	I	S
I	U	X	F	C	Z	N	G	A	Z	W	I	U	E
N	N	W	U	F	U	T	V	R	H	X	O	L	E
G	I	Z	J	H	J	R	J	L	L	V	P	O	Y
S	O	S	L	W	L	Y	L	A	Q	C	Q	X	D

Fairy Godmother

The New York Times called Dolly the 'saucy grandmother of social media' in November 2019. I'm not sure 'grandmother' is the right word, though. I'm thinking more like saucy Glinda, saucy Fairy Godmother or saucy Tinker Bell. Here she is looking like a combination of all three for you to colour in.

These are the women who *USA Today* selected as 'Women of the Century' to commemorate the 100th anniversary of the 19th Amendment to the US Constitution, which guaranteed women the right to vote in 1920. Dolly's on the list!

ENTERTAINMENT

Celia Cruz (1925–2003), salsa artist
Gloria Estefan (1957–), pop singer
Ella Fitzgerald (1917–96), jazz singer
Aretha Franklin (1942–2018), singer, songwriter
Whoopi Goldberg (1955–), actor, comedian
Katharine Hepburn (1907–2003), actor
Queen Latifah (1970–), rapper, actor
Hattie McDaniel (1893–1952), actor
Rita Moreno (1931–), Emmy, Grammy, Oscar and Tony award winner
◀ **DOLLY PARTON** (1946–)
Gertrude 'Ma' Rainey (1886–1939), blues singer
Nina Simone (1933–2003), jazz singer
Bessie Smith (1894–1937), blues singer
Anna May Wong (1905–1961), actor

POLITICS

Madeleine Albright (1937–), former Secretary of State
Florence Allen (1884–1966), first female federal judge
Shirley Chisholm (1924–2005), first Black congresswoman in America
Hillary Clinton (1947–), former US Senator, Secretary of State and First Lady
Ruth Bader Ginsburg ▶ (1933–2020), US Supreme Court justice
Barbara Jordan (1936–1996), former congresswoman
Ileana Ros-Lehtinen (1952–), first Latina elected to Congress

Wilma Mankiller (1945–2010), first female chief of the Cherokee Nation
Patsy Mink (1927–2002), first Asian-American woman elected to Congress
Michelle Obama (1964–), former First Lady
Sandra Day O'Connor (1930–), first female US Supreme Court justice
Nancy Pelosi (1940–), Speaker of the US House of Representatives
Jeannette Rankin (1880–1973), first woman elected to Congress
Condoleezza Rice (1954–), first Black female US Secretary of State
Sonia Sotomayor (1954–), first Latina Supreme Court justice
Betty Mae Tiger Jumper (1923–2011), first female chief of the Seminole Florida Tribe

CIVIL RIGHTS

Jane Addams (1860–1935), first American woman to win the Nobel Peace Prize
Alicia Garza (1981–), **Patrisse Cullors** (1983–), Opal Tometi (1984–), Black Lives Matters founders
Mary McLeod Bethune (1875–1955), education pioneer
Marca Bristo (1953–2019), disability rights activist
Ruby Bridges (1954–), civil rights activist
Tarana Burke (1973–), founder of the #MeToo movement
Marcia D. Greenberger (1946–), women's rights advocate
Fannie Lou Hamer (1917–77), civil rights activist
Dorothy Height (1912–2010), civil rights activist
Dolores Huerta (1930–), labour leader and civil rights activist
Cristina Jiménez Moreta (1984–), immigration reform advocate
Marsha P. Johnson (1945–92), LGBTQ+ activist
Helen Keller (1880–1968), disability rights activist

Bernice King (1963–), civil rights activist
Coretta Scott King (1927–2006), civil rights activist
Yuri Kochiyama (1921–2014), civil rights activist
Candace Lightner (1946–), founder of Mothers Against Drunk Driving
Felicitas Mendez (1916–88), civil rights activist
Constance Baker Motley (1921–2005), civil rights activist
Rosa Parks (1913–2005), civil rights activist
Alice Paul (1885–1977), suffragist
Frances Perkins (1880–1965), workers' rights advocate
Amelia Boynton Robinson (1911–2015), civil rights activist
Gloria Steinem (1934–), activist and feminist icon
Mary Church Terrell (1863–1954), founding member of the National Association for the Advancement of Colored People (NAACP)

Maya Lin (1959–), designer of Vietnam Veterans Memorial
Toni Morrison ▶ (1931–2019), author
Georgia O'Keeffe (1887–1986), pioneer of American modernism
Cristina Saralegui (1948–), Cuban-American editor and presenter
Amy Tan (1952–), author
Ida B. Wells (1862–1931), journalist and civil rights activist
Oprah Winfrey (1954–), former talk-show host, TV executive, actor and author
Helen Zia (1952–), journalist

SPORT

Ann Bancroft (1955–), first woman to reach the North Pole
Simone Biles (1997–), Olympic gold medallist
Bessie Coleman (1892–1926), first woman of colour to hold an international pilot's licence
Babe Didrikson (1911–56), Olympic gold medallist
Althea Gibson (1927–2003), first Black woman to win Wimbledon
Florence Griffith Joyner (1959–98), Olympic gold medallist and world's fastest woman at 100 and 200 metres
Billie Jean King (1943–), 39-time Grand Slam tennis champion, founder of the Women's Tennis Association and advocate for women's rights
Ibtihaj Muhammad (1985–), Olympic fencer
Wilma Rudolph (1940–94), Olympic gold medallist
Pat Summitt (1952–2016), University of Tennessee women's basketball coach
Serena Williams (1981–), 39-time Grand Slam tennis champion
Venus Williams (1980–), 23-time Grand Slam tennis champion

ARTS, LITERATURE AND MEDIA

Maya Angelou (1928–2014), author and activist
Julia Alvarez (1950–), award-winning author
Denise Scott Brown (1931–), architect
Lorraine Hansberry (1930–65), playwright
Zora Neale Hurston (1891–1960), novelist and anthropologist
Eunice Johnson (1916–2010), co-founder of Ebony magazine
Edna Lewis (1916–2006), chef and author

SCIENCE, MEDICINE AND EDUCATION

Virginia Apgar (1909–74), physician
Jessie 'Little Doe' Baird (1963–), linguist
Rachel Carson (1907–64), marine biologist
Anna Julia Cooper (1858–1964), education activist
Angela Davis (1944–), educator and racial justice activist
Mona Hanna-Attisha (1976–), whistleblower
Mary Jackson (1921–2005), Katherine Johnson (1918–2020) and Dorothy Vaughan (1910–2008), members of NASA's segregated mathematical unit, 'Hidden Figures'
Grace Murray Hopper (1906–92), computer programmer
Wendy Kopp (1967–), CEO of Teach for America
Antonia C. Novello (1944–), first woman to serve as Surgeon-General
Ellen Ochoa (1958–), astronaut
Sally Ride (1951–2012), astronaut

BUSINESS AND PHILANTHROPY

Aída Álvarez (1950–), first Latina to hold a Cabinet position
Mary Kay Ash (1918–2001), cosmetics executive
Nancy Brinker (1946–), founder of Susan G. Komen Foundation, one of the world's largest cancer charities
Lois Alexander Lane (1916–2007), fashion pioneer
Juliette Gordon Low (1860–1927), Girl Scouts founder
Eleanor Roosevelt (1884–1962), women's rights advocate, humanitarian and former First Lady

DOLLY AROUND THE WORLD

Dolly has been touring since the 1970s and, as well as visiting many states in the US, has visited the following countries along the way. Can you colour them in on the world map above?

CANADA

UK

IRELAND

SWEDEN

DENMARK

NORWAY

THE NETHERLANDS

GERMANY

SWITZERLAND

AUSTRALIA

NEW ZEALAND

USA

Big Break

- Aged 15, Dolly was signed as a staff songwriter by Tree Publishing Company record producer Buddy Killen. She released a single on Mercury Records called '(It May Not Kill Me But) It's Sure Gonna Hurt', but it wasn't a big success, so Dolly went back to school.

- Dolly earned cash covering songs recorded by Kitty Wells, the first female country singer to top the US Country Charts, which paid for Dolly to travel to Florida for the first time.

- Dolly became the first of her family to graduate from high school. The next day, she got on a bus to Nashville. That day, she met Carl Dean outside a laundromat in the street, and it was love at first sight!

- In the spring of 1966, Dolly and her uncle Bill were signed as staff writers to Combine Music, earning them $50 a week. They worked under record executive Fred Foster (producer of Roy Orbison's early hits) and wrote 'Put It Off Until Tomorrow', which

country star Bill Phillips recorded. It went to No. 6 in the Country Charts.

- On 30 May 1966, Dolly and Carl married in Ringgold, Georgia, in a small ceremony. Dolly kept her marriage a secret as Fred Foster had told her, 'You can't get married, because I'm going to invest all this money and this is your big shot.'

- Fred Foster gave Dolly her big break as a vocalist. She recorded 'Dumb Blonde', written by Curly Putman, which reached No. 24 on the Country Charts. It was Dolly's first hit.

- Later that year, 'Put It Off Until Tomorrow' earned Dolly and Bill a BMI Song of the Year Award. Carl accompanied Dolly to the event – the first and only time he attended a music event with Dolly.

- Dolly's debut album, *Hello, I'm Dolly,* was released in 1967. It featured a single written by

Dolly, 'Something Fishy', which broke into the Country Top 20.

- In the summer of 1967, country superstar Porter Wagoner asked Dolly to join his troupe to replace popular performer Norma Jean on the syndicated TV series *The Porter Wagoner Show.*

- Dolly signed with Porter's label, RCA Records; he became her mentor and they started recording together in the autumn. Their first album – *Just Between You and Me* – reached No. 8 on the Billboard Country Albums Chart in January 1968.

- Three months later, in April 1968, Dolly released her second solo studio album, *Just Because I'm a Woman,* and it reached No. 22.

- Later that year, at the Music City News Awards, Dolly won Most Promising Female Artist and she and Porter won Duet of the Year.

Dolly the Philanthropist

THE IMAGINATION LIBRARY

Dolly wanted to inspire every child to learn to read, so she came up with a novel idea: the Imagination Library, which she started in honour of her dad, Robert, who had never learned to read or write. Set up in 1995, the Imagination Library is a free book-gifting project distributing a book each month to children aged 0–5 registered with the programme.

To begin with, the idea was a local effort, mailing books to kids in the area Dolly grew up in, Sevier County, Tennessee. But then, the programme grew first to the whole of Tennessee, then the whole country. By 2003, the Imagination Library had delivered its one millionth book. The programme was extended to Canada in 2006 and then overseas, first to the UK in 2007, then Australia in 2013 and Ireland in 2019. By 2016, the Imagination Library was distributing one million free books a month. In 2018, Dolly presented the Imagination Library's 100 millionth book to the Library of Congress collection.

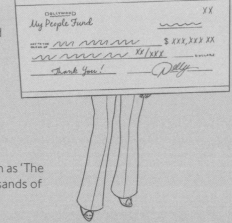

So that's why Dolly is also known as 'The Book Lady' to hundreds of thousands of kids around the world!

WHERE'S DOLLY?

Can you spot the super-mini Book Lady here among the books she's gifted to children all around the world? (Answer on page 188)

READ

The Elvis Collaboration That Wasn't

Soon after the release of Dolly's classic 1974 song 'I Will Always Love You', which was written as a farewell to her partner and mentor Porter Wagoner after Dolly made the brave decision to go solo, Elvis Presley got in touch. He wanted to record a version of the famous ballad. Great news!

And so Dolly was invited down to Elvis's studio to meet him.

But then, two days before the meeting, Dolly received a call from Colonel Tom Parker, Elvis's manager. He said, 'You do know that we have to have at least half the publishing (rights) on any song Elvis records?'

Dolly replied, 'I did not know that.'

Colonel Tom Parker: 'Well, it's just a rule.'

Dolly: 'Well, it's not my rule.'

Dolly admitted to crying all night after making the decision to turn Elvis down. She loved Elvis and was so proud that he loved the song.

In the end, Dolly's hit topped the Country Charts twice. And then there was Whitney Houston's version of the song on the soundtrack to the 1992 film *The Bodyguard*, which stayed at Number 1 for a then-record 14 weeks before going on to become one of the best-selling songs of all time … earning Dolly millions.

WORD CLOUD

COAT OF MANY COLORS ALBUM

Coat of Many Colors was Dolly's eighth solo album and was released in October 1971. It made *Rolling Stone*'s 2020 list of the 500 Greatest Albums of All Time and *Time Magazine*'s 2006 list of the 100 Greatest Albums of All Time.

The album clearly means a lot to Dolly – she said in October 2020 on *The Late Show with Stephen Colbert* that the title track was her favourite song.

LGBTQ+

'I think of myself as somebody who's just as smart as any man I know. I don't think anybody should ever be judged by whether they're male or female, black, white, blue or green. I think people should be allowed to be themselves and to show the gifts they have and be able to be acknowledged for that and to be paid accordingly.'

INTERVIEW WITH *BUST* MAGAZINE, 2015

'[Dollywood is] a place for entertainment, a place for all families, period. It's for all that. But as far as the Christians, if people want to pass judgement, they're already sinning. The sin of judging is just as bad as any other sin they might say somebody else is committing. I try to love everybody.'

ON THOSE WHO CRITICIZE LGBTQ+ PEOPLE, *BILLBOARD*, 2014

'Through the years, I've always used my femininity to my benefit. I've never slept with anybody to get to the top, though. If I slept with somebody, it's 'cause I wanted to, not to get from point A to point B.'

INTERVIEW WITH *BUST* MAGAZINE, 2015

'I think everybody should be treated with respect. I don't judge people and I try not to get too caught up in the controversy of things. I hope that everybody gets a chance to be who and what they are. I just know, if I have to pee, I'm gon' pee, wherever it's got to be.'

ON THE ISSUE OF ANTI-TRANSGENDER BATHROOM BANS, CNN, 2016

'I have a huge gay following, and I'm proud of them. Sometimes some of them look more like me than I do.'

THE NEW YORK TIMES, 2016

'Some are preachers / some are gay / some are addicts, drunks and strays / But not a one is turned away when it's family.'

'FAMILY' FROM *EAGLE WHEN SHE FLIES* ALBUM, 1991

'Sure, why can't they get married? They should suffer like the rest of us do!'

THE JOY BEHAR SHOW, 2010

'I think love is love and we have no control over that ... I think people should be allowed to [marry]. I'm not God, you know. I believe in God, I think God is the judge. I don't judge or criticize and I don't think we're supposed to.'

NEWS BREAKFAST (AUSTRALIA), 2009

'They know that I completely love and accept them, as I do all people. I've struggled enough in my life to be appreciated and understood. I've had to go against all kinds of people through the years just to be myself. I think everybody should be allowed to be who they are, and to love who they love.'

BILLBOARD, 2014

SIX DEGREES OF KEVIN BACON

Right, this game will test your knowledge of Dolly's filmography. It takes its name from the theory 'six degrees of separation' and refers to the fact that Kevin Bacon has a connection to every film ever made!

In this game, the idea is to start with Dolly herself, and work out a way of connecting her to the actor at the end of each list by linking actors via films they have both starred in. Repeat the process until you get there! (Answers on page 188)

ACTOR	FILM
1	
2 Matt Damon	

ACTOR	FILM
1	
2 Arnold Schwarzenegger	

ACTOR	FILM
1	
2 Keanu Reeves	

ACTOR	FILM
1	
2	
3 Olivia Colman	

ACTOR	FILM
1	
2	
3	
4 Meryl Streep	

Statue of Liberty

Doesn't Dolly look perfect as Lady Liberty? Although I'm not sure she'd approve of the all-green outfit, so please do Dollify her as you see fit!

KENNEDY CENTER HONOREES QUIZ: ACTORS

First presented in 1978, this annual honour is awarded to performers to recognize their significant contributions to American culture. Dolly won hers in 2006 alongside Andrew Lloyd Webber, Zubin Mehta, Smokey Robinson and Steven Spielberg.

Can you work out the actors who've been honoured from the lines they've performed? (Answers on page 188)

1 'Houston, we have a problem.'

2 'No, I am your father.'

3 'You blew it up! God damn you! Damn you all to hell!!!'

4 'Do you expect me to talk?'

5 'You talkin' to me?'

6 'Just a spoonful of sugar helps the medicine go down.'

7 'Details of your incompetence do not interest me.'

8 'I know it was you, Fredo. You broke my heart.'

9 'Get busy living or get busy dying. That's goddamn right.'

10 'Life is like a box of chocolates, Forrest. You never know what you're going to get.'

KENNEDY CENTER HONOREES QUIZ: SINGERS

Can you work out these Kennedy Center Honoree musicians from the lines they've sung? (Answers on page 188)

1 'All my troubles seemed so far away.'

2 'What's love but a second-hand emotion?'

3 'Good times never seemed so good.'

4 'It was a teenage wedding, and the old folks wished them well.'

5 'Do you believe in life after love?'

6 'If you'll be my bodyguard, I can be your long-lost pal.'

7 'Upside down / Boy, you turn me inside out.'

8 'I hear the train acomin' / It's rollin' round the bend.'

9 'I feel good, I knew that I would, now.'

10 'What you want, baby, I got it.'

Cowgirl

Dolly went full cowgirl in the publicity portraits for the 1984 film *Rhinestone*, in which she plays a country singer who turns a New York cabbie (Sylvester Stallone) into a country performer in just two weeks. While the film wasn't successful, with Stallone even 'winning' a Golden Raspberry Award for Worst Actor, he did say in 2006, 'The most fun I ever had on a movie was with Dolly Parton on *Rhinestone.*' Now that I can believe!

Here's your chance to add the finishing touches.

'DREAM MORE, LEARN MORE, CARE MORE, AND BE MORE.'

DESIGN YOUR OWN
★ DOLLY MASK ★

In April 2020, the statue of Dolly in Sevierville, Tennessee, was snapped wearing a face mask. That one was a bit basic, though – one of the disposable blue surgical ones. Nowhere near stylish enough for Dolly, so here's your chance to put that right!

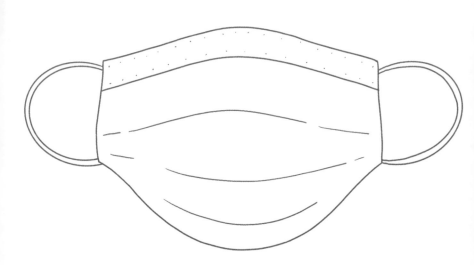

Dolly the Philanthropist
AMERICAN EAGLES

In 1990, Dollywood began a multi-year partnership with the American Eagle Foundation (AEF). The following year, the Eagle Mountain Sanctuary – a purpose-built aviary on a steep, wooded hillside designed to house disabled bald eagles that would not be able to survive in the wild – was constructed at Dollywood. It is the largest such facility in the United States. In the largest enclosure, amusingly named 'Pick a Mate', the birds are encouraged to form nesting pairs and are then moved to a private enclosure to raise their young. The hope is that their eaglets will one day be released into the wild.

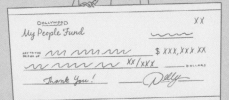

In 1992, Dollywood helped the AEF to build a 'hack' tower, from where the eagles are released into the wild. So far, between 1992 and 2019, the AEF has released 176 captive-hatched and orphaned bald eagles into the foothills of the Great Smoky Mountains. Wow!

In 2003, Dolly was given the US Fish & Wildlife Service 'Partnership Award' to recognize her support for bald eagle conservation. In 2008, Dolly was on hand to help release a bald eaglet, which had been rescued as a fallen nestling, back into the wild.

'It's a real blessing to be able to assist the foundation in its work to rescue these breathtaking birds,' she said. Bless her heart.

Dolly Pride

Dolly's public support for LGBTQ+ families goes way back to the early 1990s and her song 'Family' on the *Eagle When She Flies* album.

Her love of drag queens is legendary, and she once famously said, 'It's a good thing I was born a girl, otherwise I'd be a drag queen!' And then, in 2012, Dolly revealed that, many years ago, she'd entered a Dolly-lookalike drag contest in West Hollywood at Halloween.

To celebrate her iconic status, here's Dolly in front of a Pride flag for you to colour in!

ALL DOLLED UP

DOLLY AT THE DRIVE THRU

I've researched a lot about Dolly for this book, but this might be the thing I learned that made me smile the most. It's what she said about Sundays with Carl.

'When I'm home, I spend Sunday with my husband. If we're not cooking, we travel around in our camper, stop at fast-food restaurants and picnic. We love that stuff that will harden your arteries in a hurry.'

Digging a little deeper, I found out her restaurant of choice: Taco Bell.

'I love their tacos. They also have little pizzas that I love,' she said.

Some famous folks pretend they're regular Joes, but we know it's a fib. With Dolly, well, she really is just like the rest of us!

HOW DOES DOLLY NOT HAVE A PRESIDENTIAL MEDAL OF FREEDOM?

On 1 December 2020, Barack Obama appeared on *The Late Show with Stephen Colbert* and answered one of the most difficult questions he's ever had to face.

STEPHEN: **'How does Dolly Parton not have a Presidential Medal of Freedom*?'**

BARACK: **'That's a mistake. I'm shocked.'**

STEPHEN: **'Looking back on your eight years, do you realize that was the mistake you made?'**

BARACK: **'That was a screw-up. I'm surprised. I think I assumed that she'd already got one and that was incorrect. She deserves one!'**

STEPHEN: **'I assumed too.'**

BARACK: **'I'll call Biden.'**

It later transpired that she'd been offered it twice by the Trump administration.

'I couldn't accept it because my husband was ill, and then they asked me again about it, and I wouldn't travel because of the COVID.'

President Biden's administration reached out to her in January 2021 but she doesn't know if she's going to accept it.

'Now I feel like if I take it, I'll be doing politics, so I'm not sure!' she said.

*The Presidential Medal of Freedom, first awarded in 1963, is bestowed by the President of the USA on people who have made 'an especially meritorious contribution to the security or national interests of the United States, world peace, cultural or other significant public or private endeavors'. And Dolly needs one sharpish.

THE DOLLY PARTON CHALLENGE

On 21 January 2020, Dolly broke Instagram when she posted a collage of four squares, each one featuring a photo of Dolly as she sees herself on LinkedIn, Facebook, Instagram and Tinder. 'Get you a woman who can do it all' was the caption.

And then everyone in the world did their own with the hashtag #dollypartonchallenge.

This time, you need to draw a profile pic for each one of those four platforms. Good luck!

LINKEDIN

FACEBOOK

INSTAGRAM

TINDER

Celebrity Fans

It's rare to find a superstar who counts fellow stars as her superfans, but hey, that's Dolly!

'This is my hero, musical and personal hero of all time, beautiful person inside and out and the person who I always wanted to grow up to be.'

SHANIA TWAIN

'It was just amazing to get to see her work and see her write new lyrics down on a paper plate, you know, after lunch, and everyone would be trying to take that paper plate home with them! She's amazing.'

ALLISON JANNEY

'I have great respect for her as a businesswoman to start with, and secondly as an artist. She's a great songwriter, a great singer and she's been a good friend and that's all you can ask from anyone.'

KENNY ROGERS

'She's the most special person in the world ... I've ever met. Anyone, whether they've come in contact with her personally or not or just listened to her music or just watch her, no one doesn't like Dolly, and that's because I think people see the way she'll treat anyone, here in this room, the way she'd treat her biggest fan, the way she'd treat her worst enemy, it's all the same. Super-respectful and love. I've had such a great role model as a musician but also as a person. She is just the kindest of all.'

MILEY CYRUS

'She's more than I possibly thought she could be.'

QUEEN LATIFAH

'After many, many years of doing this show, I finally feel like a real talk-show host because you are here. I remember how great you were on Johnny Carson, so charming and talented and all that stuff, and now you're right here before me.'

JIMMY KIMMEL, INTRODUCING DOLLY FOR THE FIRST TIME ON HIS SHOW

'She was so supportive and wonderful. Dolly's Dolly. There'll never be another one like that. Wow – she's just terrific. Great to be with. Great fun.'

BURT REYNOLDS

Miss Piggy to Dolly:
'You do not just have millions of fans. You have millions of friends!'

Dolly:
'I'm flattered, but you also have millions of fans.'

Miss Piggy (outraged):
'Millions? We're talking BILLIONS, Dolly.'

'No one really knows the total gem of a soul that Dolly Parton is. I love her.'

SALLY FIELD

'Like a lot of little girls in the South, I grew up loving Dolly Parton. Every Sunday night, I'd stay up and watch her variety show with my mother, mouthing all the words to every single one of her songs. So I guess you could say I didn't just love Dolly, I wanted to be Dolly. This dignified, spiritual and very caring woman also happens to be a real hoot. Her laugh is just infectious.'

REESE WITHERSPOON

Can you spot the super-mini Queen of Country here among the creatures of her beloved Great Smoky Mountains? (Answer on page 188)

WHERE'S DOLLY?

ALL DOLLED UP

Rhinestones

Dolly dazzles in rhinestones, doesn't she? Now it's your chance to embellish her outfit with the colours you'd like to see Dolly wear!

Solo Success

- Dolly became a member of the Grand Ole Opry cast in 1969 and earned her first Grammy nomination in 1970 in the category Best Country Vocal Performance, Female.

- Dolly and Porter won Vocal Duo of the Year at the CMA Awards and the Music City News Awards in 1970. They repeated the win at the CMAs the following year.

- In 1971, Dolly scored her first solo No. 1 hit on the Billboard Country Chart with 'Joshua'. Later that year, she released 'Coat of Many Colors' about the childhood coat her mother had made her, which reached No. 4 in the charts.

- Dolly's star was rising and Porter's was fading. When she originally agreed to work with him, she said she'd only do it for five years. But in 1973, after seven years, she decided to leave. Anticipating a negative reaction from a meeting with Porter, instead Dolly wrote a song to tell him how she felt. She went into his office and said, 'Porter, sit down. I want to sing you a song I wrote.' That song was 'I Will Always Love You'. Porter started to cry and told her it was the best song she'd written. He said he wouldn't stand in her way if he could produce the record. Dolly said, 'It's a deal!'

- Possibly that same day, or certainly within the next few days, Dolly wrote 'Jolene',

which topped the Country Charts, earning Dolly her second solo No. 1. It also became an international hit, topping the Canadian Country Charts and reaching No. 7 on the UK Singles Chart.

- 'I Will Always Love You' was released in March 1974 as the second single from her album *Jolene*. It hit the No. 1 spot on the Country Charts in June.

- In 1975, Dolly won Female Vocalist of the Year at the CMAs, an award she'd been nominated for in six of the previous seven years. She repeated the feat the following year.

- In 1977, Dolly was crowned Entertainer of the Year at the Academy of Country Music Awards and Entertainer of the Year at the CMAs the following year.

- Also in 1977, Dolly scores her first No. 1 album, *New Harvest ... First Gathering*, which was also the first album she produced herself. She followed it up eight months later with *Here You Come Again*, which also topped the charts and became the first Dolly album to be certified platinum by the Recording Industry Association of America (RIAA).

- Capping off quite a decade, in 1979 Dolly won her first Grammy in the category Best Vocal Performance, Female, for the album *Here You Come Again*.

DOLLY'S DUETS

In addition to being
a legendary solo artist and one-third
of an all-star trio, Dolly has also performed some
of the most memorable duets of all time. I've put
'Islands in the Stream' at the top, FOR GOOD REASON.

'Islands in the Stream'
with Kenny Rogers

'Rockin' Years' with Ricky Van Shelton

'When You Tell Me That You Love Me'
with Julio Iglesias

'He's Everything' with Queen Latifah

**'Everything's Beautiful (In Its
Own Way)'** with Willie Nelson

'I Really Don't Want to Know'
with Willie Nelson

'Creepin' In' with Norah Jones

'From Here to the Moon and Back'
with Kris Kristofferson

'I Know You By Heart'
with Smokey Robinson

'Words' with Barry Gibb

'When I Get Where I'm Going'
with Brad Paisley

'Just Someone I Used to Know'
with Porter Wagoner

'I Will Always Love You' with Vince Gill

'There Was Jesus' with Zach Williams

As an honourable mention, she also appears on the song 'Faith'
by Galantis feat. Mr Probz. You might be surprised to hear that
she appears on an EDM track by a Swedish electronic duo.
I have to admit I was. But I was also ecstatic.

The first time I heard it, on an EDM shuffle playlist while I was out
running, I actually stopped running, stupefied by the thought,
'That can't really be Dolly, can it?!!!' And then, there she was on the
YouTube video, as a glamorous bus driver, giving it her everything,
as you'd expect, and spreading love and joy far and wide.

Now it gets me out of the house for a run even when it's freezing outside!

Setting the Record Straight: 'JOLENE'

There are a fair few urban legends floating around about Dolly, so here's the truth, straight from the horse's mouth.

WAS JOLENE BASED ON A REAL PERSON?

… (drum roll)

YUP!

The name 'Jolene' was really inspired by a girl who asked Dolly for her autograph after a show in the late 1960s.

'Would you sign this to Jolene?' she asked.

'Jolene — that's a beautiful name. I bet you're named after your daddy. Is his name Joe?' asked Dolly.

'No, it's just Jolene,' said the little girl.

'Well, I love that name, and if you ever hear a song with it, you'll know it's about you.'

In order to keep the name in her head, Dolly kept repeating 'Jolene' on the tour bus. And that gave her the thought: *Why don't I just start the song like that?*

The story behind the song was based on Carl flirting with a beautiful red-headed bank teller at a branch close to where Dolly and Carl were living before they got married.

'He was spending more time at the bank than we had money,' Dolly told Jimmy Fallon on The Tonight Show. **'And I thought, well, that ain't gonna work out too good!'**

BEST-SELLING SINGLES OF ALL TIME

The 10 best-selling singles of all time, in terms of estimated physical copies sold (remember when that was a thing!) are:

SONG	ARTIST	WRITER	COPIES (million)	YEAR
'White Christmas'	Bing Crosby	Irving Berlin	50	1942
'Candle in the Wind 1997'	Elton John	Elton John and Bernie Taupin	33	1997
'Rock Around the Clock'	Bill Haley & His Comets	Max C. Freedman and James E. Myers	25	1954
'I Will Always Love You'	Whitney Houston	**Dolly Parton**	20	1992
'It's Now or Never'	Elvis Presley	Aaron Schroeder and Wally Gold	20	1960
'We Are the World'	USA for Africa	Michael Jackson and Lionel Richie	20	1985
'My Heart Will Go On'	Celine Dion	Will Jennings and James Horner	18	1997
'All I Want for Christmas Is You'	Mariah Carey	Mariah Carey and Walter Afanasieff	16	1994
'(Everything I Do) I Do it for You'	Bryan Adams	Bryan Adams, Michael Kamen, and Robert John Lange	15	1991
'You're the One That I Want'	John Travolta and Olivia Newton-John	John Farrar	15	1978

NOTE: Total sales are notoriously difficult to verify. According to some sources, the following three singles could be added to the list: Mungo Jerry's 1970 hit 'In the Summertime', with an estimated 30 million copies; The Ink Spots' 1939 hit 'If I Didn't Care', with an estimated 19 million copies; and Baccara's 'Yes Sir, I can Boogie', with an estimated 18 million copies.

Dolly Pinball

A special edition Dolly pinball machine (with all the bells and whistles you'd expect) was made in 1976 by the manufacturer Bally. Have a go at colouring in this one inspired by Dolly.

Love and Dreams

'I met him the day I got to Nashville back in 1964. I wasn't a star then, so I've never had to worry that he loves me because I'm a star and I've got money or make money or whatever. I know he loves me for me, and that means a lot to me.'

TALKING ABOUT CARL IN AN INTERVIEW WITH OPRAH, 2010

'I know every line in his face and he knows every hair in my wig.'

ON CARL, *TODAY* SHOW, 2014

'I ain't near where I'm goin'. My dreams are far too big to stop now 'cause I ain't the greatest at what I do, but I become greater because I believe.'

INTERVIEW WITH *ROLLING STONE*, 1977

'I've been fortunate enough to see dreams come true, in my case, but I have paid my dues. I always say I'm going to give God the credit but I definitely want the cash.'

INTERVIEW WITH *DIGITAL JOURNAL*, 2014

'We just gotta do our best day-to-day, be the best person we can, do the best work we can, and just keep on dreamin'.'

INTERVIEW WITH
MASHABLE, 2015

'He's always loved who I was, and I loved who he was, and we never tried to change each other.'

DISCUSSING HER HUSBAND CARL IN
O, THE OPRAH MAGAZINE, 2016

'Carl says he'd think less of any man who didn't fall in love with me.'

INTERVIEW WITH THE
DAILY MAIL, 2011

'You can wish your life away. But if you're going to dream, you're going to have to get out and put some wings on them dreams, and some feet and fingers and some hands. You can't just sit around and think of all the things you want to do. You've got to think of what you want to do, and then you've got to get out and make it happen.'

INTERVIEW WITH
SOUTHERN LIVING, 2016

'I wake up with new dreams every day.'

INTERVIEW WITH
MASHABLE, 2015

If I had it to do all over, I'd do it all over again. I'm dragging him kicking and screaming into the next 50 years. Wish us luck!'

ON CELEBRATING HER 50TH WEDDING ANNIVERSARY IN 2016

DOLLY DOES TWITTER

Dolly's got over 5 million followers on Twitter but she only follows 43 people (as of February 2021). Can you guess who the following 10 are from the cryptic clues? (Answers on page 188)

1 ET's favourite confectionary maker has what's needed to eat dessert

2 Subsistence pugilists

3 This type of musical theatre doesn't lose when it's gratis

4 Possessive US department store in fifty shades

5 Tarzan's other half is keen on you

6 This rubber ring is turning in flight

7 French father plus a Z stays at a plush hotel chain

8 11th letter finds a peg on the golf course and tucks into some pear cider

9 Barbie's partner's joint is run by Buck's family

10 Casual James trips over at length

DOLLY IS OFFICIALLY A WORLD-BEATER!

In January 2018, Dolly added another couple of awards to what is most probably a shelf creaking under the weight of trophies. But these ones are slightly different. She's now officially a Guinness World Record holder. Twice over!

She was recognized for two incredible feats:

⊙ Most decades (6) with a Top 20 hit on the Billboard's Hot Country Songs Chart

⊙ Most hits on theBillboard's Hot Country Songs Chart by a female artist

Dolly was presented with the certificates in Nashville and sat down for an interview.

'To receive these two Guinness World Records is so great. Joining so many wonderful singers and songwriters who have been honoured this way feels so special to me. You never know when you start out with your work how it's going to turn out, but to have these two world records makes me feel very humbled and blessed!'

'9 TO 5': A 'WORKING FROM HOME' SPECIAL EDITION

Well, I tumble outta bed and stumble to the kitchen

Pour myself a couple of gins (and hoover up the last
of the banana bread)

Jump in the shower and the blood starts pumping,

But out on the street, the traffic isn't jumping

Cos folks like me are working 9 to 5 (at home)

Working 9 to 5 (at home), what a way to make a living

Barely getting by on Zoom and that's no kidding

You just lose your mind and the kids drain your credit

It's enough to drive you crazy if you let it!

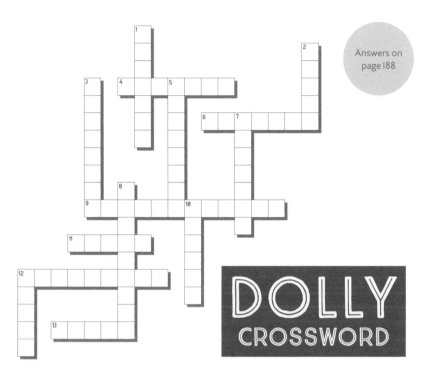

Answers on page 188

DOLLY CROSSWORD

ACROSS

4 The Glastonbury stage Dolly played in 2014 (7)

6 What is the second-largest city in Tennessee? (clue: Walking in) (7)

9 Dolly's 2019 Netflix drama about the memories and inspirations behind her songs (12)

11 The first name of Dolly's singer-songwriter brother, who passed away in January 2021 (5)

12 Which genre of music did Dolly branch into in 1999 with the album *The Grass Is Blue*? (9)

13 First name of the actor that Dolly gave her blessing to in 2018 to play her if a biopic about Dolly ever happens (5)

DOWN

1 Dolly had turned down numerous offers to appear nude in which magazine? (7)

2 The surname of Dolly's goddaughter (5)

3 Which wedding anniversary did Dolly and Carl celebrate in 2016? (8)

5 What is Dolly's star sign? (8)

7 The name of the COVID-19 vaccine Dolly's donation helped to fund (7)

8 The famous American bird species Dolly has helped protect (9)

10 The surname of the actor who played office supervisor Violet Newstead in *9 to 5* (6)

12 Which bear is found in the Great Smoky Mountains National Park? (5)

DOLLY'S BIRTHDAY QUIZ

Dolly shares her birthday – 19 January – with some other famous folks.
Can you guess who they are from the tricky clues?
(Answers on pages 188–9)

1 19th–century French artist, renowned for his *Card Players* series of paintings

2 Swedish men's tennis player who won Wimbledon twice, in 1988 and 1990

3 The younger half of a country–influenced rock 'n' roll duo whose first hit was 'Bye Bye Love' in 1957

4 19th–century short–story writer and poet most famous for his narrative poem 'The Raven'

5 Scottish pioneer of the Industrial Revolution associated with steam engines; the unit of power is named after him

6 US singer–songwriter who topped the chart posthumously in 1971 with the hit 'Me and Bobby McGee'

7 British racing driver who won the 2009 Formula One World Champtionship

8 Former BBC journalist who famously interviewed Princess Diana in 1995

9 Current US Secretary of Transportation who became the first openly gay person to launch a presidential campaign in 2020, eventually dropping out and endorsing Joe Biden

10 Author of *Strangers on a Train* and *The Talented Mr Ripley*

HOW DOLLY MET CARL

This sounds like a Hollywood rom-com script but sometimes life imitates art!

Dolly first met Carl Dean outside the amazingly named Wishy Washy Laundromat in Nashville, Tennessee. She had just graduated from high school on a Friday night in 1964 and left for Nashville the following morning to pursue her dreams of being a country music star. Here's how Dolly described what happened that afternoon.

'I was walking down the street to the laundromat, and he stopped me. He said, "Hey, you're going to get sunburned out here!"'

Recalling the day when discussing their 50th wedding anniversary in 2016, she said: **'I was surprised and delighted that while he talked to me, he looked at my face — a rare thing for me. He seemed to be genuinely interested in finding out who I was and what I was about.'**

Meanwhile, what was going through Carl's head? Well, luckily for us (seeing as he's a man who doesn't like the limelight), he shared this at their golden wedding celebration.

'My first thought was, "I'm gonna marry that girl." My second thought was, "Lord, she's good-lookin'." And that was the day my life began,' Carl said.

Bless!

ALL DOLLED UP

Have a Jolly Dolly Christmas

Dolly released the album *A Holly Dolly Christmas* in 2020 to make everyone feel better at the end of what was a pretty terrible year. So here's a festive colouring-in page – don't hold back on the colour!

WORD CLOUD
9 TO 5 AND ODD JOBS ALBUM

Here are the words that appear most frequently in Dolly's most famous album!

SPOT THE DOLLY DIFFERENCE

Can you spot the seven differences between this illustration of Dolly and the one opposite? (Answers on page 189)

WOODROW WILSON AWARD WINNERS

Woodrow Wilson was the 28th President of the USA and best known for being the architect behind the League of Nations. Founded in 1920 after the Paris Peace Conference, the League of Nations was the first intergovernmental organization dedicated towards maintaining world peace. The awards were established in 1999 and now recognize prominent leaders, thinkers and activists around the world. Can you match up the roles with the people they belong to? (Answers on page 189)

ROLE	PERSON
President of Brazil (2011–16)	John McCain
Architect behind the Guggenheim Museum in Bilbao	Andrew Lloyd Webber
US Secretary of State (2001–05)	Betty Ford
Commander of US Central Command (2008–10)	Hillary Clinton
Legendary composer of musicals	Colin L. Powell
Multiple Grammy-award-winning superstar	Jack Nicklaus
Prime Minister of Australia (1996–2007)	Frank Gehry
First Lady of the USA (1974–77)	David Petraeus
Male golfer with the most Major Championship wins	Dilma Rousseff
Long-serving Arizona senator and former navy officer	John Howard
First woman nominated by a major political party for President	**Dolly Parton**

DOLLY'S FAMILY TREE

GRANDPARENTS (maternal)

Rena Kansas Valentine
1902 – 1968 🦋 (married 1919)

Rev. Jacob Robert 'Jake' Owens
1899 – 1992 🦋

GRANDPARENTS (paternal)

Bessie Elizabeth Rayfield
1898 – 1975 🦋 (married 1912)

William 'Walter' Parton
1888 – 1982 🦋

— MOTHER —

Avie Lee Caroline Owens
1923 – 2003 🦋 (married 1939)

— FATHER —

Robert Lee Parton
1921 – 2000 🦋

Willadeene
1940 –
Author of Parton family memoir: Smoky Mountain Memories: Stories from the Hearts of the Parton Family, 1996

David Wilburn
1942 –

Coy Denver
1943 –

Dolly Rebecca
1946 –

Bobby Lee
1948 –

Stella Mae
1949 –
Also a country singer and songwriter, whose biggest hit was the 1975 song 'I Want to Hold You in My Dreams Tonight'; she appeared in 2015's Coat of Many Colors

Cassie Nan
1951 –
Performed in the Dollywood show 'My People' in 2013

Randel 'Randy' Huston
1953 – 2021 🦋
Country singer-songwriter who sang a song on the Rhinestone soundtrack and had two Top 40 US Country Chart hits

Larry Gerald
1955 🦋
Died shortly after being born

Estel Floyd
1957 – 2018 🦋
Songwriter who wrote and performed many songs for Dolly including the duet 'Rockin' Years', which Dolly sang with Ricky Van Shelton in 1991

Freida Estelle
1957 –
Former singer turned minister and owner of a wedding chapel in Sevierville

Rachel Ann
1959 –
former actor who appeared on the ABC sitcom version of 9 to 5

Appearances

'I hope people see the brain underneath the wig and the heart beneath the boobs.'

INTERVIEW WITH GEORGE STROUMBOULOPOULOS, 2012

'People always say, "But you always look so happy." Well, that's Botox! Nobody's happy all the time. But I work hard at it.'

DREAM MORE: CELEBRATE THE DREAMER IN YOU

'My nails are my rhythm section when I'm writing a song all alone. Someday, I may cut an album, just me and my nails.'

INTERVIEW WITH ROGER EBERT, 1980

'I've been around a long time. Long enough for people to realize that there's more to me than the big hair and the phoney stuff.'

INTERVIEW WITH *THE GUARDIAN*, 2014

'I want people to know it's me when they see me coming and when they see me leavin'. So I figured I might as well look even more extreme.'

DOLLY ON DOLLY: INTERVIEWS AND ENCOUNTERS WITH DOLLY PARTON, EDITED BY RANDY L. SCHMIDT, CHICAGO REVIEW PRESS, 2017

'I look totally artificial, but I am totally real, as a writer, as a professional, as a human being. A rhinestone shines just as good as a diamond.'

INTERVIEW WITH *ELLE* MAGAZINE, 2019

'People know I have no taste. No style, no class. If I have any class, it's all low. No matter how I dress, I'm still going to look cheap.'

INTERVIEW WITH *THE TIMES*, 2020

'I just wanted to be pretty. I wanted to be striking. I wanted to be colourful. I wanted to be seen. When I went to Nashville, I always overdid it. When they say, "Less is more", I say, "That's BS. More is more!"'

INTERVIEW WITH *ELLE* MAGAZINE, 2019

'I'm outgoing on the inside, so I felt I needed to be flamboyant on the outside.'

INTERVIEW WITH *THE TIMES*, 2020

'People ask me how long it takes to do my hair. I don't know, I'm never there.'

INTERVIEW WITH *HARPER'S BAZAAR*, 2016

WORD CLOUD

HERE YOU COME AGAIN ALBUM

Here are the words that appear most frequently in *Here You Come Again* – Dolly's first album to sell a million copies and gain platinum certification by the Recording Industry Association of America.

MUSICARES PERSON OF THE YEAR

In 2019, Dolly made history again. She became the MusiCares Person of the Year, awarded by the charity branch of The Recording Academy to recognize musicians not only for their artistic merit but also for their commitment to philanthropy. She became the first country music star to receive the honour.

In a tribute concert hosted by Little Big Town, Pink sang 'Jolene', Yolanda Adams sang 'I Will Always Love You', Miley Cyrus, Mark Ronson and Shawn Mendes performed 'Islands in the Stream' and Kacey Musgraves and Katy Perry rocked Dolly-inspired outfits to sing 'Here You Come Again'. The evening even featured a reunion of Dolly, Linda Ronstadt and Emmylou Harris. Wowzers!

When accepting the award, Dolly said: 'It's been such a thrill for me tonight to see all these great artists singing songs I've written or been a part of. Watching them is sort of like watching porn. You're not personally involved but you still get off on it!'

The other recipients of the prestigious award are:

1991	David Crosby	2001	Paul Simon	2011	Barbra Streisand
1992	Bonnie Raitt	2002	Billy Joel	2012	Paul McCartney
1993	Natalie Cole	2003	Bono	2013	Bruce Springsteen
1994	Gloria Estefan	2004	Sting	2014	Carole King
1995	Tony Bennett	2005	Brian Wilson	2015	Bob Dylan
1996	Quincy Jones	2006	James Taylor	2016	Lionel Richie
1997	Phil Collins	2007	Don Henley	2017	Tom Petty
1998	Luciano Pavarotti	2008	Aretha Franklin	2018	Fleetwood Mac
1999	Stevie Wonder	2009	Neil Diamond	2019	**Dolly Parton**
2000	Elton John	2010	Neil Young	2020	Aerosmith

★ Honorary Muppet ★

Dolly's had a long history with the Muppets and *Sesame Street* created two Muppets in her honour – Dolly Pardon (who featured on *The Count Counts* record album) and Polly Darton (a country singer who eventually gained a couple of back-up dog singers).

In 1986, Dolly even received a coveted Honorary Muppet Award, which, according to Muppet Wiki, has only been given to 'the select individuals who have achieved a place in Muppet History as someone who has appeared in Muppet form, have gained muppet [acting] parts, or been described by the Muppets as somewhat Muppet-like'.

These esteemed folks include: Goldie Hawn, Peter Ustinov, Robin Williams, Pee-Wee Herman, Louie Anderson, Jon Voight, Cee Lo Green and Ricky Gervais.

But few folks can claim to have gone on a date with Kermit the Frog, something Dolly did in 1988.

Well, Kermit was half an hour late and Dolly went looking for him, finding her date in a bar backstage (of all places) drinking Perrier and ordering a second bowl of flies from the barman. He told Dolly he was 'kinda depressed' at being called Kermit **the Frog**, pointing out (quite fairly) that Dolly wasn't called 'Dolly the Human'.

'Why do we have to have labels?' he asked.

'Well, so we can get the right clothes back from the laundry,' Dolly said, chirpily, which cheered him up.

He warned her, 'If you kiss me, there's no prince. This is as good as it gets.'

Love it!

They reunited in November 2012 for a duet of 'Islands in the Stream'.

DESIGN YOUR OWN
DOLLY MICROPHONE

Dolly made her first 'microphone' herself – it was an old tin can balanced on a tobacco stick wedged in between planks of her front porch. Inspired by Dolly's creativity, have a go at embellishing the stand and the mike with your own design!

COUNTRY MUSIC HALL OF FAME

Here are the names of the select few country stars that have been inducted into the Country Music Hall of Fame – the highest honour a country music professional can be awarded.

1961
Jimmie Rodgers
Fred Rose
Hank Williams

1962
Roy Acuff

1964
Tex Ritter

1965
Ernest Tubb

1966
Eddy Arnold
James R. 'Jim' Denny
George D. Hay
Uncle David Macon

1967
Red Foley
Joseph Lee ('J.L.') Frank
Jim Reeves
Stephen Sholes

1968
Bob Wills

1969
Gene Autry

1970
The Carter Family
Bill Monroe

1971
Arthur E. Satherley

1972
Jimmie Davis

1973
Chet Atkins
Patsy Cline

1974
Owen Bradley
Pee Wee King

1975
Minnie Pearl

1976
Paul Cohen
Kitty Wells

1977
Merle Travis

1978
Grandpa Jones

1979
Hubert Long
Hank Snow

1980
Johnny Cash
Connie B. Gay
Sons of the Pioneers

1981
Vernon Dalhart
Grant Turner

1982
Lefty Frizzell
Roy Horton
Marty Robbins

1983
Little Jimmy Dickens

1984
Ralph Peer
Floyd Tillman

1985
Flatt and Scruggs

1986
The Duke of Paducah
('Whitey' Ford)
Wesley Rose

1987
Rod Brasfield

1988
Loretta Lynn
Roy Rogers

1989
Jack Stapp
Cliffie Stone
Hank Thompson

1990
Tennessee Ernie Ford

1991
Felice and Boudleaux
Bryant

1992
George Jones
Frances Preston

1993
Willie Nelson

1994
Merle Haggard

1995
Roger Miller
Jo Walker-Meador

1996
Patsy Montana
Buck Owens
Ray Price

1997
Harlan Howard
Brenda Lee
Cindy Walker

1998
George Morgan
Elvis Presley
E.W. 'Bud' Wendell
Tammy Wynette

1999
Johnny Bond
Dolly Parton
Conway Twitty

2000
Charley Pride
Faron Young

2001
Bill Anderson
The Delmore Brothers
The Everly Brothers
Don Gibson
Homer and Jethro
Waylon Jennings
The Jordanaires
Don Law
The Louvin Brothers
Ken Nelson
Sam Phillips
Webb Pierce

2002
Bill Carlisle
Porter Wagoner

2003
Floyd Cramer
Carl Smith

2004
Jim Foglesong
Kris Kristofferson

2005
Alabama
DeFord Bailey
Glen Campbell

2006
Harold Bradley
Sonny James
George Strait

2007
Ralph Emery
Vince Gill
Mel Tillis

2008
Tom T. Hall
Emmylou Harris
The Statler Brothers
Ernest V. 'Pop' Stoneman

2009
Roy Clark
Barbara Mandrell
Charlie McCoy

2010
Jimmy Dean
Ferlin Husky
Billy Sherrill
Don Williams

2011
Bobby Braddock
Reba McEntire
Jean Shepard

2012
Garth Brooks
Hargus 'Pig' Robbins
Connie Smith

2013
Bobby Bare
Cowboy Jack Clement
Kenny Rogers

2014
Hank Cochran
Ronnie Milsap
Mac Wiseman

2015
Jim Ed Brown and The
Browns
Grady Martin
The Oak Ridge Boys

2016
Charlie Daniels
Fred Foster
Randy Travis

2017
Alan Jackson
Jerry Reed
Don Schlitz

2018
Johnny Gimble
Ricky Skaggs
Dottie West

2019
Jerry Bradley
Brooks & Dunn
Ray Stevens

2020
Dean Dillon
Marty Stuart
Hank Williams Jr

Popularity of the Name 'JOLENE'

After the song's release, the name 'Jolene' climbed to the 245th most popular girl's name (it rose from the 562nd most popular girl's name in 1973). After dipping again in the late 1990s, it's now climbing again, reaching the 449th most popular name in 2019 (which is 1 in every 2,649 baby girls).

Author of *The Baby Name Wizard*, Laura Wattenberg, puts it down to 'both the appeal of the name and the appeal of the sound. Jolene features two long vowel sounds, which are highly prized in contemporary name style.'

Sadly, the name 'Dolly' has been on a steady decline since 1950, when it was the 491st most popular girl's name. Now only 1 out of every 34,393 baby girls are named Dolly!

So Dolly still has cause for concern from Jolene!

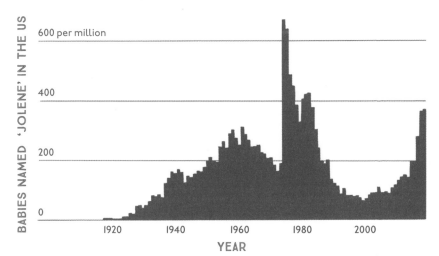

BABIES NAMED 'JOLENE' IN THE US

600 per million

400

200

0

1920   1940   1960   1980   2000

YEAR

★ GRAND OLE ★
OPRY

So what is this Grand Ole Opry place that country folks talk about?

In short, it's the home of country music.

It's a weekly stage concert in Nashville, Tennessee, that began its life as the WSM Barn Dance in the fifth-floor radio studio of the National Life & Accident Insurance Company on 28 November 1925. Now it's the longest-running radio broadcast in the history of the US.

It wasn't until 10 December 1927 that the words 'Grand Ole Opry' were uttered together in a live radio broadcast by presenter George Hay. The show immediately followed a programme featuring classical music and opera, so Hay opened with: 'For the past hour, we have been listening to music largely from Grand Opera, but from now on, we will present "The Grand Ole Opry".' The name stuck.

The original venue proved too small, so, after several relocations, in June 1943, the Opry moved to the Ryman Auditorium, which would become known as the 'mother church of country music'.

In 1974, the Opry took up residence in the newly constructed Grand Ole Opry House, which featured a 6ft circle of hardwood cut out from the Ryman and placed in the centre of the Grand Ole Opry stage. The next evening, President Nixon appeared on stage.

Dolly made her Opry debut in 1959 aged just 13 alongside her uncle Bill Owens and received three encores. Wonderfully, it was Johnny Cash who introduced her:

'We've got a little girl here from up in East Tennessee. Her daddy's listening to the radio at home and she's gonna be in real trouble if she doesn't sing tonight, so let's bring her out here.'

Dolly's Morning Routine

So, it may surprise you to learn that Dolly does not work 9 to 5.

Here's a little glimpse into her morning schedule as revealed to *Marie Claire* in December 2020.

 **3am (!):** Dolly wakes up and says a morning prayer, asking God to 'bless the day and bring all the right things'.

 3–7am: Dolly gets straight to work, writing, replying to emails and working on her forthcoming projects. 'I get more work done during that little period of time when the world is calm, energies are down, and I just feel like a farmer,' she said.

 7am: Dolly cooks breakfast for her and Carl, wearing high heels (Dolly, not Carl, presumably). Apparently their breakfast is usually quite healthy but can involve sausage patties and biscuits and gravy (best to look this up for the full visual effect if you're not from the US).

She also divulged that *lights out* happens around 10pm. Well, that's her aim. Usually it's a little later and she gets by on three hours' sleep, occasionally making up for it with a power nap during the day. Good going!

DOLLY'S BEAUTY RITUALS

Dolly's feelings about beauty, the refreshingly self-deprecating way she perceives herself and her awareness of how she's perceived are all legendary.

We know that her commitment to make-up borders on the religious. Here's what she told Oprah Winfrey:

'The only way I'd be caught without my make-up is if my radio fell in the bathtub while I was taking a bath and electrocuted me and I was in between make-up at home. I hope my husband would slap a little lipstick on me before he took me to the morgue.'

On skincare, sometimes tried and tested is the way forward:

'I try all the new things that come out, but there's nothing better than good old Vaseline® and those Almay eye make-up remover pads.'

We know that she's a big fan of wigs:

'My own hair is so flat and fine. I could never make it do anything – that's why I wear wigs. I think God gave me talent cos he screwed up my hair.'

'I've got better things to do than count them. But I wear one every day of the week, so probably 365.'

Here's how she feels about Botox and plastic surgery:

'Thanks to Botox and fillers, as well as the work that I've already had, my face pretty much maintains itself. I look at myself like a show dog. I've got to keep her clipped and trimmed and in good shape!'

And my personal favourite:

'If I have one more facelift, I'll have a beard!'

EGOT QUIZ

Only 16 people have won a 'grand slam' of show business, winning an Emmy, Grammy, Oscar and a Tony award – the four awards honouring achievements in television, music, film and theatre. A further five people have won all four if you count honorary awards, which we are for the sake of this quiz.

So your task is to work out who these legends are from the length of their names and the letters we've filled in for you. (Answers on page 189)

1   A_D__Y H_____N

2   _IT_ M____NO

3   J__N G__L__D

4   M__ _R_O_S

5   _HOO_ _ G_____G

6   J___ _EG__D

7   _A__RA S_____S__D

8   L__A M__N___I

9   _AM_S E___ J___S

10 A____W LL___ W____R

WHERE'S DOLLY?

See if you can spot the super-mini Dolly here among this kaleidoscope of butterflies. (Answers on page 189)

WALK OF FAME QUIZ

You'd think one Hollywood Walk of Fame Star was enough, particularly as you're expected to pay the $30,000 fee for the ceremony, but some folks have more than one, including our own Dolly – one as a solo artist and one for her collaboration with Emmylou Harris and Linda Ronstadt. Can you guess these iconic multiple-star figures from the clues?
(Answers on page 189)

DOLLY PARTON

DOLLY PARTON

1 Legendary comedian who has hosted the Academy Awards more than anyone else

2 This Merseyside musician was born Richard Starkey

3 'That's Amore' crooner

4 First ex-Beatle to score a No. 1 single

5 Rat Pack legend who was famously investigated by the FBI for alleged links to the Mafia

6 Lead singer of The Supremes

7 Fronted the skiffle group The Quarrymen before going on to greater things

8 Motown legend who co-wrote and sang 'The Tears of a Clown'

9 Won a record eight Grammy Awards in a single year, in 1984

10 Sang the best-selling single of all time

'IF YOU DON'T LIKE THE ROAD YOU'RE WALKING, START PAVING ANOTHER ONE.'

Dolly the Philanthropist
2016
GREAT SMOKY
MOUNTAIN WILDFIRES

Beginning on 23 November 2016, a series of wildfires devastated areas of the Great Smoky Mountains National Park in Tennessee, claiming 14 lives and injuring nearly 200. Around 14,000 residents and tourists had to evacuate and over 2,400 buildings were either destroyed or badly damaged.

Dolly, being the superhero she is, set up the My People Fund on 28 November. A total of $8.9 million was raised through star-studded telethons featuring Dolly, Kenny Rogers and Cyndi Lauper among others. Four days later, each family whose home had been destroyed or damaged beyond repair was given $1,000 per month for five months (with a final payment of $5,000 in the sixth month), sourced from a combination of outside donations and contributions from the Dollywood Foundation.

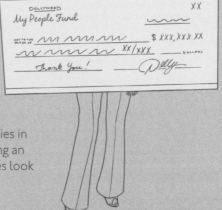

Dolly's My People Fund also launched a partnership with the Mountain Tough Recovery Team to continue supporting families in the months that followed, providing an additional $3 million. She sure does look after folks, doesn't she?

Doing a Degree in Dolly

In 2017 it became possible to take your Dolly love to the next level and complete a college course about her life!

University of Tennessee history professor Dr Lynn Sacco had heard Dolly give the commencement address at the university in 2009 and it gave her an idea: why not propose a course on Dolly's life?

And so, in 2017 'Dolly's America: From Sevierville to the World' was offered as an option to history students. The course description explained that students would learn 'how a "hillbilly" girl from Appalachia grew up to become an international one-word sensation'.

The course spawned the *Dolly Parton's America* podcast, hosted by Jad Abumrad, which was touted as the top podcast of 2019 by Forbes. Dr Sacco and her students appeared in two episodes and the team involved in the podcast even won a prestigious Peabody Award that year, which recognizes excellence in broadcasting.

Sadly, Dolly's America is not being offered as an online course to the general public yet. But watch this space!

Setting the Record Straight:

ALL IN A DAY'S WORK

There are a fair few urban legends floating around about Dolly, so here's the truth, straight from the horse's mouth.

DID DOLLY REALLY WRITE 'I WILL ALWAYS LOVE YOU' AND 'JOLENE' ON THE SAME DAY IN 1973?

… (drum roll)

QUITE PROBABLY!

Dolly explains in *Dolly Parton: Songteller* that it's possible they were written on the same day. When she was looking through a bunch of old cassette recordings, she found them on the same tape so she '… might have written "Jolene" later that night'. She went on to explain that the fact they appeared on the same cassette tape means that they must have been written within the same time frame, otherwise she would have used another cassette.

Not bad going!

WORD CLOUD

EAGLE WHEN SHE FLIES ALBUM

Here are the words that appear most frequently in Dolly's 1991 album *Eagle When She Flies* – her first album since *9 to 5 and Odd Jobs* to top the US Country Charts. It went platinum the following year.

DESIGN YOUR OWN DOLLY TENNESSEE LICENSE PLATE

The great state of Tennessee has commissioned you to design a Dolly Parton-inspired license plate, to be fitted to all new cars. Do Dolly proud!

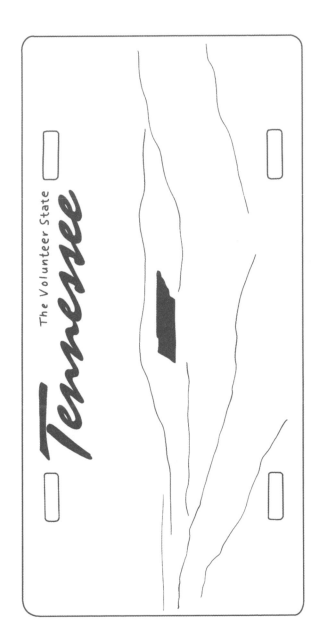

DOLLY BOGGLE™

See how many words you can make out of the Dolly-inspired board below. (Answers on pages 189–90)

T	H	E	I
R	O	N	B
U	T	T	E
R	F	L	Y

Superstardom

- In 1980, Jane Fonda cast Dolly in the office-based comedy film *9 to 5* to play Doralee Rhodes. Dolly also wrote the film's theme song in her head on set before going back to her hotel each night and getting it down on paper.

- '9 to 5' came out on 3 November 1980, the lead single from Dolly's concept album *9 to 5 and Odd Jobs*. The song reached No. 1 on the Country Chart in January 1981 and the top of the Pop Charts in February, making it Dolly's biggest hit so far. It was certified gold that month, selling over 500,000 copies.

- The film *9 to 5*, released in December 1980, was a huge success, becoming the third-biggest box office hit of 1981 in the US after the blockbusters *Raiders of the Lost Ark* and *Superman II*.

- *9 to 5* later became a television sitcom, running from 1982–88, with Dolly's sister Rachel Dennison being cast as Doralee.

- The single '9 to 5' earned Dolly her first Academy Award nomination for Best Original Song, but she lost out to 'Fame' from *Fame* in the ceremony in March 1981.

- In February 1982, Dolly won two Grammy awards, for Best Country Song and Best Vocal Performance, Female, for '9 to 5'. The album scored her another Grammy nomination.

- Dolly was cast as the lead in the comic musical *The Best Little Whorehouse in Texas* in 1982 alongside Burt Reynolds. She was nominated for a Golden Globe for Best Actress in a Motion Picture (Comedy or Musical) for her role as Miss Mona Stangley, but lost out to Julie Andrews for her performance in *Victor/Victoria*.

- 'I Will Always Love You' appeared in the movie and on the soundtrack for *The Best Little Whorehouse in Texas*. Released as a single in July 1982, it topped the Country Charts again, earning Dolly the rare honour of having the same song top the charts twice.

- The duet 'Islands in the Stream', written and originally performed by the Bee Gees, was recorded by Dolly and Kenny Rogers. Released in 1983, it topped both the Country and Pop Charts, also becoming No. 1 in Australia, Austria and Canada. The song eventually was certified platinum, selling two million copies.

- Dolly was awarded a star on the Hollywood Walk of Fame in 1984.

- In 1986, Dolly became a co-owner of Silver Dollar City, Tennessee, which changed its name to Dollywood.

- Long-time friends and country stars Dolly, Emmylou Harris and Linda Ronstadt recorded a collaborative album together. *Trio* was released in March 1987, peaked at No. 1 on the Country Chart for 5 weeks and reached No. 6 in the Pop Charts.

- *Trio* won a Grammy in 1988 for Best Country Performance by a Duo or Group with Vocal. The album also won Vocal Event of the Year at the 1988 CMAs.

GLASTONBURY HEADLINERS QUIZ

Glastonbury's legendary Pyramid Stage first appeared in 1971, made of metal sheeting and conceived as a one-tenth replica of the Great Pyramid of Giza. Dolly famously graced the stage in 2014 and despite the sea of mud the site had become, she played the most famous outdoor stage in the world in a sparkling white pantsuit. That's how you do it!

Can you work out the following artists or bands who have played the Pyramid Stage from the clues? (Answers on page 190)

1 Reached No. 1 in the UK Albums Chart with *Different Class* in 1995

2 Former lead singer of Destiny's Child

3 First Black British solo act to play the Pyramid Stage

4 Four guys named Followill

5 Born Shawn Corey Carter

6 Representing the South 'in The Battle of Britpop'

7 Founded by a former member of Nirvana

8 The highest-selling Aussie artist of all time

9 Won an Oscar in 2012 for Best Original Song — the first Bond theme to do so

10 'The Boss' of the E Street Band

ALL DOLLED UP

Stars and Stripes

Here's an easy one to colour in! Dolly wore this sparkling, shimmering, stars-and-stripes blazer as a 4 July outfit and shared it in 2019.

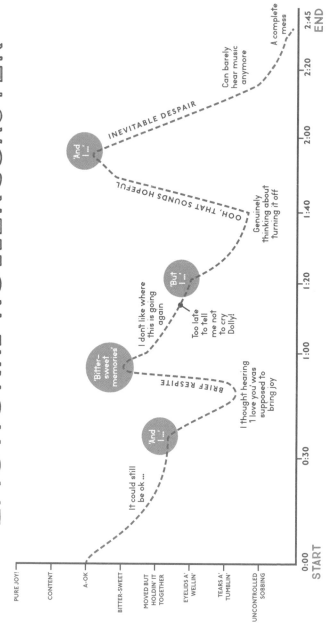

'I Will Always Love You'
EMOTIONAL ROLLERCOASTER

PURE JOY!
CONTENT
A-OK
BITTER-SWEET
MOVED BUT HOLDIN' IT TOGETHER
EYELIDS A' WELLIN'
TEARS A' TUMBLIN'
UNCONTROLLED SOBBING

0:00 START · 0:30 · 1:00 · 1:20 · 1:40 · 2:00 · 2:20 · 2:45 END

It could still be ok ...

'And I ...'

I thought hearing 'I love you' was supposed to bring joy

BRIEF RESPITE

'Bitter-sweet memories'

I don't like where this is going again

Too late to tell me not to cry Dolly!

'But I ...'

OOH, THAT SOUNDS HOPEFUL

Genuinely thinking about turning it off

'And I ...'

INEVITABLE DESPAIR

Can barely hear music anymore

A complete mess

DESIGN YOUR OWN DOLLY BILL

When the good folks at the Federal Reserve decide to give George Washington a break as the face of the $1 bill, why not replace him with a Dolly dollar bill – it's meant to be! So, let's do Dolly proud and design a banknote she'd love.

DOLLY CROSSWORD

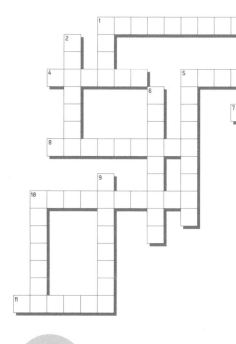

ACROSS

1 The winged creature that Dolly is most associated with (9)

4 Dolly's first number one single (clue: shares its name with a tree that U2 sang about) (6)

5 The number of kids Dolly's parents had (6)

7 The number of Grammy Awards Dolly has won for songs, albums and performances (3)

8 The city in which you'll find the Grand Ole Opry (9)

10 The name of the 1984 movie she starred in with Sylvester Stallone (10)

11 Surname of one of Dolly's other Trio members (6)

DOWN

1 President who awarded her the Kennedy Center Honors in 2006 (4)

2 The state that Dolly and Carl got married in (7)

3 Dolly's husband's surname (4)

5 The name of Dolly's home state (9)

6 The name of Dolly's amusement park (9)

9 Surname of her co-star in *The Best Little Whorehouse in Texas* (8)

10 Dolly's middle name, which she shares with the title of a famous Daphne Du Maurier novel (7)

Answers on page 190

DOLLY BINGO

Sit yourself down, watch a Dolly interview on YouTube and cross out the boxes when each one of the following occurs!

Dolly emits a high-pitched giggle	Says 'Country'	Starts answering a question with 'Well'	Says 'I sure am'
Dolly places one hand on top of the other	Says 'You better believe it'	Dolly gestures just south of the collar bone	You can hear the sound of Dolly's nails tapping
Dolly touches her interviewer playfully	Dolly starts flirtin'!	Says 'Southern gal'	Spontaneously breaks into song
Plays a prank on the interviewer	Fires off a disarming one-liner	You spot a rhinestone!	Makes interviewer laugh uncontrollably

123

Femininity and Feminism

'I was the first woman to burn my bra; it took the fire department four days to put it out.'

TWITTER, 2010

'God tells us not to judge one another, no matter what anyone's sexual preferences are or if they're black, brown or purple. And if someone doesn't believe what I believe, tough shit.'

ON EQUALITY IN AN INTERVIEW WITH *THE GUARDIAN*, 2011

'I've never thought of myself as a feminist. I've used my femininity and sexuality as a weapon and a tool ... but that's just natural.'

INTERVIEW WITH *THE TIMES*, 2013

'It [the film] really paved the way and things did change but there's still a lot more to be done. With ... people drawing attention again to equal pay, equal work, harassment in the workplace, this is just another good way for us to shine a light on some things that need to be lit up a little.'

SPEAKING TO REUTERS ON THE RED CARPET AHEAD OF THE OPENING PERFORMANCE OF '9 TO 5 THE MUSICAL' IN LONDON, FEBRUARY 2019

'I try to encourage women to be all that they can be and I try to encourage men to let us be that.'

INTERVIEW WITH *BUST* MAGAZINE, 2015

'You don't have to look like everybody else. You don't have to be a raving beauty to be special and to be beautiful.'

GOOD MORNING AMERICA INTERVIEW WITH JENNIFER ANISTON, 2018

'I've been fortunate in my life that my being a girl kind of helped me along the way, and being from a strong family of men, and women, I'd never be afraid to stand on my own or to say, "Go to hell", if that's where you needed to go.'

INTERVIEW WITH *ELLE* MAGAZINE, 2019

'I never met a man whose rear I couldn't kick if he didn't treat me with the right respect.'

ACCEPTING THE MUSICARES PERSON OF THE YEAR AWARD, 2019

'If I'm not a good example of a woman in power, I don't know who is. I don't have to preach. I write it. I sing it. I live it. I'm out there just promoting mankind, but I am most definitely going to get behind those gals.'

ON GENDER EQUALITY, INTERVIEW WITH *ELLE* MAGAZINE, 2019

'I still believe that women should get paid equal and should be treated with respect. I'm all about that. I don't get out and have to preach it or march in the streets, I write about it.'

INTERVIEW WITH ABC, 2019

★ DOLLIPOP ★

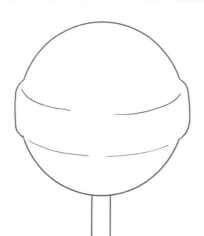

'Dollipop, Dollipop,
Oh Dolly, Dolly, Dolly …'

That feels better, although you've got that song stuck in your head now!

So which type of lollipop would Dolly go for? A Dollipop of many colours? A butterfly design? One in the shape of a clock face with the numbers 9 and 5? The possibilities are endless!

Dolly the Philanthropist
TENNESSEE HOSPITALS

Dolly has made a number of generous contributions towards Tennessee hospitals.

May 2007 – Dolly raises $500,000 at a benefit concert to fund the LeConte Medical Center in Sevier County, a new hospital and cancer treatment centre. A further $250,000 was contributed both by Dollywood and Dolly Parton's Stampede Dinner Attraction. The new hospital opened its doors in 2010 and named its women's health department the Dolly Parton Center for Women's Services.

October 2017 – Dolly donates $1 million to the Monroe Carell Jr. Children's Hospital Vanderbilt. The money went towards the hospital's paediatric cancer programme, which treated Dolly's niece Hannah Dennison for four years starting in 1993. Dolly visited the hospital and sang songs from her new children's album, *I Believe in You*, including 'Chemo Hero', written about Hannah. All proceeds from the album went towards the Imagination Library.

May 2018 – Dolly and her niece Hannah unveil a new addition to the Vanderbilt hospital – The Hannah Dennison Butterfly Garden. Jeff Balser, President and CEO of the Vanderbilt University Medical Center, said:

'Dolly's symbol is the butterfly, so it only seems fitting that The Hannah Dennison Butterfly Garden will become a focal point of our hospital, offering patients and families important respite while they are here.'

Collaborations and Hall of Fame

- In 1989, Dolly had two No. 1 singles, 'Why'd You Come in Here Lookin' Like That' and 'Yellow Roses' from the album *White Limozeen*, which spent 100 weeks on the Country Chart, peaking at No. 3. It was later certified gold by the RIAA.

- 'Rockin' Years', a duet between Dolly and Ricky Van Shelton, was released in February 1991 as the first single on Dolly's album *Eagle When She Flies*. It topped the Country Charts and was later certified platinum. In late 1991, Dolly embarked on what would be her last major tour for a decade.

- In 1992, Whitney Houston recorded a cover of Dolly's 'I Will Always Love You' for the soundtrack to the smash-hit film *The Bodyguard.* It spent a then record-breaking 14 weeks at the top of the Billboard Hot 100 Chart and became one of the best-selling singles of all time.

- In 1994 Dolly wrote a memoir entitled *Dolly: My Life and Other Unfinished Business,* which spent two months on *The New York Times* bestseller's list.

- In 1995, Dolly launched Imagination Library, her free book-gifting programme for children up to the age of five.

- Dolly and Vince Gill recorded a duet of 'I Will Always Love You' for her 1995 album *Something Special*. It earned them a Grammy nomination for Best Country Collaboration with Vocals in 1995 and won them Vocal Event of the Year at the 1996 CMA Awards.

- In February 1999, Dolly, Emmylou Harris and Linda Ronstadt released their second collaborative album, *Trio II*, which reached No. 4 on the Country Chart. The single 'After the Gold Rush' won the Grammy for Best Country Collaboration with Vocals and Video Event of the Year at the CMT Video Awards.

- In September 1999, Dolly received the highest honour in country music by being inducted into the Country Music Hall of Fame during the CMA Awards. During her acceptance speech, she paid tribute to Porter Wagoner.

- In October that year, Dolly released her first bluegrass album, called *The Grass is Blue*. It earned her a Grammy for Best Bluegrass Album in 2001.

- Dolly was inducted into the National Academy of Popular Music/Songwriters Hall of Fame in June 2001. Emmylou Harris performed at the ceremony.

- Dolly's second bluegrass album, *Little Sparrow*, was nominated for Best Bluegrass Album in 2002 and the single 'Shine' won Best Female Vocal Performance at the Grammys.

'I'VE ALWAYS BEEN MISUNDERSTOOD BECAUSE OF HOW I LOOK. DON'T JUDGE ME BY THE COVER 'CAUSE I'M A REAL GOOD BOOK!'

★ Nicknames ★

Dolly's earned a fair few nicknames in her career.
Here are the most well-known:

The Smoky Mountain Nightingale

Her first nickname, and her favourite, which she got as a 10-year-old working on
the *The Cas Walker Farm and Home Show*. She's also known as
The Smoky Mountain Songbird.

The Iron Butterfly

Named for her love of butterflies but also her business savvy, for having the
strength of mind and courage to break away from Porter Wagoner at the right
moment and for saying no to Elvis's manager's demands.

Backwoods Barbie

Sounds faintly offensive, but it's actually a self-proclaimed nickname and
Dolly used it proudly for the name of her 42nd solo studio album.

The Book Lady

Many kids around the world know Dolly as 'The Book Lady' due to her wonderful
Imagination Library book-gifting programme.

Aunt Granny

Nickname that Dolly's nephews and nieces know her by. Their kids call her
'GeeGee'.

One she doesn't like at all is **'The Queen of Country'**.
In 2018, Dolly said on *Nightline* that the

'Queen of country music is Kitty Wells.
And there are others like Loretta and Tammy!'

DOLLY
BOGGLE™

See how many words you can make out of the Dolly-inspired board below. (Answers on page 190)

D	O	L	L
Y	P	A	R
T	O	N	I
S	A	C	E

TOP 20 RICHEST SINGERS IN THE WORLD

According to *Smooth Radio*, as of September 2020, these are the richest 20 singers in the world

NAME	NET WORTH	POSITION
Paul McCartney	$1.2 billion	1
Bono	$700 million	2
Madonna	$590 million	3
Mariah Carey	$520 million	4
Elton John	$500 million	5
Dolly Parton	$500 million	6
Gloria Estefan	$500 million	7
Bruce Springsteen	$500 million	8
Victoria Beckham	$450 million	9
Shania Twain	$450 million	10
Celine Dion	$430 million	11
Jon Bon Jovi	$410 million	12
Johnny Mathis	$400 million	13
Barbra Streisand	$400 million	14
Jennifer Lopez	$380 million	15
Toby Keith	$365 million	16
Mick Jagger	$360 million	17
Beyoncé	$355 million	18
Ringo Starr	$350 million	19
Katy Perry	$330 million	20

WORD CLOUD

BACKWOODS BARBIE ALBUM

Backwoods Barbie was the first album released on Dolly's own label, Dolly Records, in 2008.

It was her 40th solo studio album and was accompanied by a tour across North America and northern Europe that kept on expanding due to public demand. After she returned from the European leg of the tour in August, though, something peculiar happened. Rumours suddenly began to circulate on the internet that Dolly had died of congestive heart failure. No one was more surprised than Dolly herself, who, in characteristic Dolly style, later said, 'I did about have a heart attack when I found out I was dead.' Amazing.

WHERE'S DOLLY?

See if you can spot the super-mini Queen of Country here in this guitar shop! (Answer on page 190)

NEW

BEST!

Music

DESIGN YOUR OWN DOLLY TATTOO

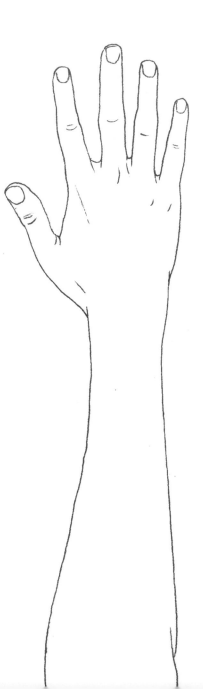

The subject of Dolly's tattoos has been the source of speculation for years. Jay Leno famously asked her about them on his show in 1999 and caught a glimpse of a butterfly and an angel on her upper arm through a cut-out in her dress. In 2020, Dolly was a guest on a podcast with Jad Abumrad, who'd been requested by students at the University of Tennessee to ask Dolly about them. She said:

'I'm very fair–skinned and when I have any kind of surgery or any kind of scarring, it discolours. When I first started getting a few little things done, I had a few little tattoos to cover up some scarring. But they're very delicate. I don't have the dark ones. They're all pastel [colours]. I have some butterflies, I have some lace and some little bows — a couple things like that!'

Here's your chance to design as many tattoos for Dolly as you want. You know what she likes by now!

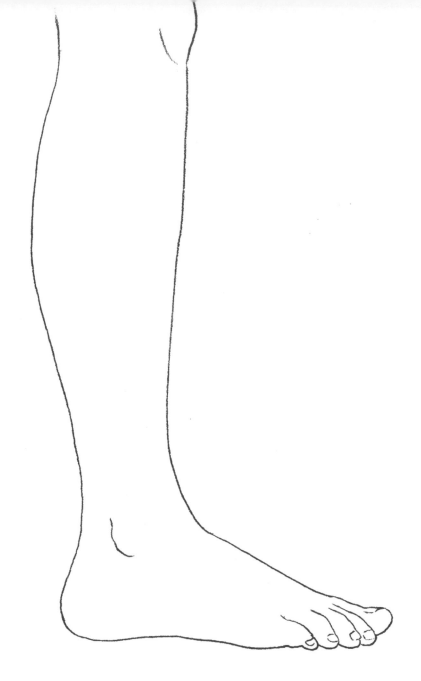

SPOT THE DOLLY DIFFERENCE

Can you spot the seven differences between this illustration
of Dolly and the one opposite? (Answers on page 190)

Dolly the Sheep

In July 1996, a sheep was cloned at the University of Edinburgh's Roslin Institute from the cells of an adult sheep. She was named Dolly and became the most famous clone in history.

So why was she called Dolly? Well, the reason is a bit cheeky.

It turns out the name choice came from an impromptu remark from John Bracken, an anaesthetist at the Roslin Institute who was there when Dolly was born and looked after her for the whole of her life.

'When Dolly was born I said we should call this sheep Dolly, simply because she had been cloned from an adult mammary cell. And I don't think I need to say any more!' he said.

Here's what Dolly (Parton) had to say about it in an interview with the *Daily Record* in 2014 before she played a concert in Glasgow.

'I was told she was called after me because she had big mammary glands. She gave me a lot of competition but I heard that when they first named her they used the mammary glands for cloning and the scientist who came up with that thought he had to name her Dolly. I never met her, but I always said there's no such thing as baaad publicity.'

INSURED BODY PARTS

According to MSN.com, the following celebrities have insured their body parts, voice or smile. From this table, it sounds like Dolly is selling herself short (!), although that figure was from the 1970s …

CELEBRITY	BODY PART/FEATURE	INSURANCE VALUE
Dolly Parton	Breasts	$600,000
Rihanna	Legs	$1 million
Heidi Klum	Legs	$2 million
Madonna	Breasts	$2 million
Keith Richards	Hands	$2 million
Kylie Minogue	Bum	$5 million
Bruce Springsteen	Voice	$6 million
Daniel Craig	Whole body	$9.5 million
America Ferrera	Smile	$10 million
Jennifer Lopez	Bum	$27 million
Julia Roberts	Teeth	$30 million
David Beckham	Legs	$70 million
Cristiano Ronaldo	Legs	$144 million
Mariah Carey	Legs	$1 billion

DOLLY BIOGRAPHY

Honours

- In July 2002, Dolly released *Halos & Horns*, the third of her bluegrass albums, and embarked on a 25-show tour of the US and UK.

- Chasing Rainbows, a museum based on Dolly's life, opened in Dollywood in 2002.

- In 2003, Dolly was presented with the BMI (Broadcast Music, Inc.) Icon award, awarded to 'songwriters to honor their unique and indelible influence on generations of music makers'.

- Also that year, a tribute album was recorded in Dolly's honour, which included Alison Krauss singing '9 to 5', Norah Jones with 'The Grass is Blue' and Krauss and Shania Twain singing 'Coat of Many Colors'.

- In December 2003, Dolly was named No. 4 in the CMT Greatest Women in Country Music, with only Patsy Cline, Tammy Wynette and Loretta Lynn above her.

- Dolly was honoured as a Living Legend by the Library of Congress in 2004 for her significant contribution to the cultural heritage of the USA.

- In October 2005, Dolly returned to the top of the Country Charts, singing with Brad Paisley on 'When I Get Where I'm Going'.

- In November 2005, Dolly received the National Medal of Arts, which is awarded to those '… deserving of special recognition by reason of their outstanding contributions to the excellence, growth, support and availability of the arts in the United States'.

- In March 2006, Dolly received a second Oscar nomination for Best Original Song, this time for 'Travelin' Thru' from the soundtrack to *Transamerica*, a film about a trans woman who takes a road trip with a boy claiming to be her son. The song also garnered Golden Globe and Grammy nominations.

- In December 2006, Dolly was awarded Kennedy Center Honors, which celebrates 'the contributions and careers of artists who have left an indelible mark on our shared American culture and character'.

- In 2009, Dolly was inducted into the Gospel Music Hall of Fame and the Music City Walk of Fame, both in Nashville.

- In 2010, Dolly accepted the Applause Award, the most prestigious award in the amusement park industry, on behalf of Dollywood.

Flower Power

Dolly really rocked the flower-power look in the 1960s with the long sleeves and flares. Can you give her a bit of trademark colour, glitz and glam?

Dolly's Wedding to Carl

On 30 May 1966,
just two years after meeting in
the street outside the Wishy Washy Laundromat
in Nashville, Dolly Parton and Carl Dean got married.

Soon after they met, Carl was called up for military service, serving two years in the army. The two kept in touch and got engaged after Dean returned. Dolly's record label, Monument, wanted her to hold off on a marriage for a while, especially as they had marketed her as a bubble-gum pop singer and were fearful of the negative impact on her career. Dolly's response: 'I ain't waitin'!'

So Dolly (aged 20) and Carl (23) hopped across the Tennessee state border to Ringgold, Georgia. There they found a Baptist church and asked the preacher, Pastor Don Duvall, if he'd marry them. The only people there were the preacher and his wife and Dolly's mama Avie Lee, who had made Dolly a little white dress and a wedding bouquet and brought along a little Bible. They kept news of their nuptials secret for a whole year!

WHERE'S DOLLY?

See if you can spot the super-mini Dolly here among her adoring fans!
(Answer on page 190)

Setting the Record Straight:

LOOKALIKE CONTEST

There are a fair few urban legends floating around about Dolly, so here's the truth, straight from the horse's mouth.

DID DOLLY REALLY LOSE A DOLLY PARTON LOOKALIKE CONTEST?

… (drum roll)

SHE SURE DID!

Dolly revealed the truth in her 2012 book *Dream More* and spoke about it during interviews with Oprah and ABC's *Nightline* show.

It was a drag-queen celebrity lookalike contest in Los Angeles.

'I just kind of over-exaggerated everything I am – bigger hair, bigger beauty marks, bigger boobs, if you can imagine!' Dolly said.

'All these beautiful drag queens had worked for weeks and months getting their clothes. So I just got in the line and I just walked across … but I got the least applause.'

Songwriting

'My songs are the door to every dream I've ever had and every success I've ever achieved.'

'My guitar is like my best friend, and my songs are like my therapy ... some days I'll write four or five songs. Some days I'll write one. They're almost always spinning in my head.'

INTERVIEW WITH ALISON BONAGURO OF CMT.COM, 2016

'In the early days, Porter would not exactly scold me, but he'd say, "You're writing too many damn verses. You're makin' these songs too damn long." And I'd say, "Yeah, but I'm tellin' a story. I have a story to tell."'

INTERVIEW WITH *AMERICAN SONGWRITER*, 2008

'If something sounds familiar, I think, "Oh my goodness, what is that?" Then I'll track it down and, in my case, it's usually just one of my own songs!'

ON PLAGIARISM, INTERVIEW WITH THE BBC, 2016

'Everything's a song to me. Anything that happens, any conversation I have, somebody'll say somethin', I think, "Oooh, that's a good idea for a song.'"

INTERVIEW WITH DAN RATHER, 2014

'My songs are like my children and I expect them to support me when I'm old.'

INTERVIEW WITH *BUST* MAGAZINE, 2015

'I'm a songwriter, so I have to live with my feelings on my sleeve. I have to not harden my heart, because I want to stay open to feel things. So when I hurt, I hurt all over. And when I cry, I cry real hard. And when I'm mad, I'm mad all over. But I was born with a happy heart. I'm always looking for things to be better.'

INTERVIEW WITH *SOUTHERN LIVING*, 2014

'It's so fulfilling to think that I could actually leave something in the world today that wasn't there yesterday.'

INTERVIEW WITH ALISON BONAGURO OF CMT.COM, 2016

'I don't need a therapist, 'cos I write it out. If I've got something bothering me, I just get it out. If I'm mad, I write that. If I'm hurt, I write that. If I'm happy, I write that. I write what I feel. That's my doctor.'

INTERVIEW WITH *THE TIMES*, 2015

'I'll write on anything. If I come up with an idea, [I'll take] whatever is in my pocketbook [even] if it's the last receipt I got from the drive thru at McDonald's.'

INTERVIEW WITH *BUSTLE*, 2020

Cowboy Boots

Dolly's lost her favourite cowboy boots and needs you to design a pair that she'll love pronto before her next gig!

DESIGN DOLLY'S SUPERHERO COSTUME

Everyone knows that Dolly is a superhero: a philanthropist, an inspiring businesswoman, a champion of equal rights and someone who always seems to find the right words to say at the right time. She's someone that *everybody* loves. And that's a rarity. For me, there's only one other person on that level: David Attenborough. Wow, that would be a fun dinner party!

Such is Dolly's universal intergenerational popularity that *The New York Times* wrote an article in November 2019 entitled, 'Is there anything we can all agree on? Yes – Dolly Parton'. Damn right.

So with all that in mind, the task comes to you to design her superhero costume.

NATIONAL MEDAL OF ARTS WINNERS

Created by the US Congress in 1984, the National Medal of Arts is the highest award for artists and patrons of the arts. The medals are given by the President at an event each year.

Can you guess the names of the recipients from their famous work/famous character they've played? (Answers on page 191)

1 Playwright:
Death of a Salesman

6 Actor:
Michael Corleone

2 Singer:
'Georgia on My Mind'

7 Actor:
Ellis Boyd 'Red' Redding

3 Poet:
'On the Pulse of Morning'

8 Director:
Star Wars

4 Singer:
'Blowin' in the Wind'

9 Singer:
'Evergreen'

5 Writer:
To Kill a Mockingbird

10 Actor:
Jessica Fletcher

★ DOLLY DOES AMERICA ★

These are all the states that Dolly has performed in and the year that she first performed there. Can you colour them in on the map?

1959 Tennessee	**1985** Florida
1972 Oregon	**1985** Indiana
1973 Georgia	**1985** Massachusetts
1973 Illinois	**1985** Kentucky
1975 Virginia	**1985** West Virginia
1976 Wisconsin	**1985** Utah
1977 California	**1985** Arizona
1977 Colorado	**1985** New Mexico
1977 Texas	**1985** Washington
1977 Missouri	**1989** Kansas
1977 New York	**1990** Minnesota
1978 Michigan	**1992** North Carolina
1978 Ohio	**2002** South Dakota
1978 New Jersey	**2004** Idaho
1978 Rhode Island	**2004** Connecticut
1978 Mississippi	**2004** Nebraska
1978 Louisiana	**2004** South Carolina
1979 Maryland	**2005** Arkansas
1979 Pennsylvania	**2005** Oklahoma
1981 Nevada	**2005** Iowa
1982 Alabama	**2005** Maine

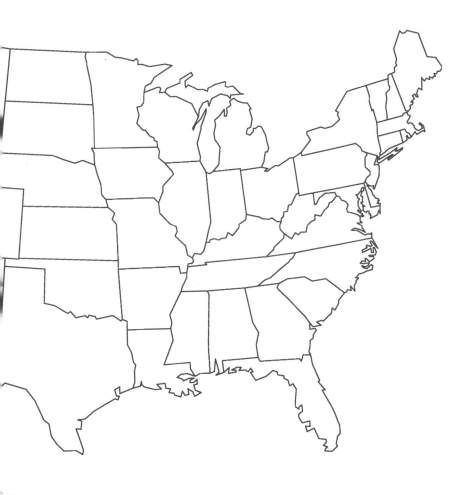

155

SONGWRITERS HALL OF FAME

1970
Fred E. Ahlert
Ernest Ball
Katharine Lee Bates
Irving Berlin
William Billings
James A. Bland
James Brockman
Lew Brown
Nacio Herb Brown
Alfred Bryan
Joe Burke
Johnny Burke
Anne Caldwell
Harry Carroll
Sidney Clare
George M. Cohan
Con Conrad
Sam Coslow
Hart Pease Danks
Reginald De Koven
Peter De Rose
Buddy De Sylva
Mort Dixon
Walter Donaldson
Paul Dresser
Dave Dreyer
Al Dubin
Vernon Duke
Gus Edwards (The
    Star Maker)
Raymond B. Egan
Daniel Decatur
    Emmett
Ted Fiorito
Fred Fisher
Stephen Foster
George Gershwin
L. Wolfe Gilbert
Patrick Gilmore
Mack Gordon
Ferde Grofe
Woody Guthrie
Oscar
    Hammerstein II
W. C. Handy
James F. Hanley
Otto Harbach
Charles K. Harris
Lorenz Hart
Ray Henderson
Victor Herbert
Billy Hill
Joseph E. Howard
Julia Ward Howe
Carrie Jacobs-Bond
Howard Johnson

James P. Johnson
James Weldon
    Johnson
Arthur Johnston
Isham Jones
Scott Joplin
Irving Kahal
Gus Kahn
Bert Kalmar
Jerome Kern
Francis Scott Key
Lead Belly
Sam M. Lewis
Frank Loesser
Ballard MacDonald
Edward Madden
Joseph McCarthy
Jimmy McHugh
George W. Meyer
James V. Monaco
Neil Moret
Theodore F. Morse
Lewis F. Muir
Ethelbert Nevin
Jack Norworth
Chauncey Olcott
John Howard
    Payne
James Pierpont
Lew Pollack
Cole Porter
Ralph Rainger
Harry Revel
Eben E. Rexford
Jimmie Rodgers
Richard Rodgers
Sigmund Romberg
George F. Root
Billy Rose
Vincent Rose
Harry Ruby
Bob Russell
Jean Schwartz
Harry B. Smith
Samuel Francis
    Smith
Ted Snyder
John Philip Sousa
Andrew B. Sterling
Harry Tierney
Charles Tobias
Roy Turk
Egbert Van Alstyne
Albert Von Tilzer
Harry Von Tilzer
Fats Waller
Samuel A. Ward

Kurt Weill
Percy Wenrich
Richard A. Whiting
Clarence Williams
Hank Williams
Spencer Williams
Septimus (Sep)
    Winner
Harry M. Woods
Henry Clay Work
Allie Wrubel
Vincent Youmans

1971
Harold Arlen
Hoagy Carmichael
Duke Ellington
Dorothy Fields
Rudolf Friml
Ira Gershwin
Alan Jay Lerner
Johnny Mercer
Jimmy Van Heusen
Harry Warren

1972
Harold Adamson
Milton Ager
Burt Bacharach
Leonard Bernstein
Jerry Bock
Irving Caesar
Sammy Cahn
J. Fred Coots
Hal David
Howard Dietz
Sammy Fain
Arthur Freed
Haven Gillespie
John Green
Yip Harburg
Sheldon Harnick
Ted Koehler
Burton Lane
Edgar Leslie
Frederick Loewe
Joseph Meyer
Mitchell Parish
Andy Razaf
Leo Robin
Arthur Schwartz
Pete Seeger
Carl Sigman
Jule Styne
Ned Washington
Mabel Wayne
Paul Francis

Webster
Jack Yellen

1975
Louis Alter
Mack David
Benny Davis
Edward Eliscu
Bud Green
Lou Handman
Edward Heyman
Jack Lawrence
Stephen Sondheim

1977
Ray Evans
Jay Livingston

1980
Alan Bergman
Marilyn Bergman
Betty Comden
Adolph Green
Herb Magidson

1981
Cy Coleman
Jerry Livingston
Johnny Marks

1982
Rube Bloom
Bob Dylan
Jerry Herman
Gordon Jenkins
Harold Rome
Jerry Ross
Paul Simon
Al Stillman
Meredith Willson

1983
Harry Akst
Ralph Blane
Ervin Drake
Fred Ebb
Bob Hilliard
John Kander
Hugh Martin
Neil Sedaka
Harry Tobias
Alec Wilder
Stevie Wonder

1984
Richard Adler
Bennie Benjamin

Neil Diamond
Norman Gimbel
Al Hoffman
Henry Mancini
Maceo Pinkard
Billy Strayhorn
George David Weiss

1985
Saul Chaplin
Gene De Paul
Kris Kristofferson
Jerry Leiber
Carolyn Leigh
Don Raye
Fred Rose
Mike Stoller
Charles Strouse

1986
Chuck Berry
Boudleaux Bryant
Felice Bryant
Marvin Hamlisch
Buddy Holly
Jimmy Webb

1987
Sam Cooke
Gerry Goffin
Carole King
John Lennon
Barry Mann
Paul McCartney
Bob Merrill
Carole Bayer
    Sager
Cynthia Weil

1988
Leroy Anderson
Noël Coward
Lamont Dozier
Brian Holland
Eddie Holland

1989
Lee Adams
Leslie Bricusse
Eddie DeLange
Anthony Newley
Roy Orbison

1990
Jim Croce
Michel Legrand
Smokey Robinson

1991
Jeff Barry
Otis Blackwell
Howard Greenfield
Ellie Greenwich
Antônio Carlos
  Jobim

1992
Linda Creed
Billy Joel
Elton John
Mort 'Doc' Pomus
Mort Shuman
Bernie Taupin

1993
Paul Anka
Mick Jagger (The
  Rolling Stones)
Bert Kaempfert
Herb Rehbein
Keith Richards
  (The Rolling
  Stones)

1994
Barry Gibb
  (Bee Gees)
Maurice Gibb
  (Bee Gees)
Robin Gibb
  (Bee Gees)
Otis Redding
Lionel Richie
Carly Simon

1995
Bob Crewe
Kenneth Gamble
Bob Gaudio
Leon Huff
Andrew Lloyd
  Webber
Max Steiner

1996
Charles Aznavour
John Denver
Ray Noble

1997
Harlan Howard
Jimmy Kennedy
Ernesto Lecuona
Joni Mitchell
Phil Spector

1998
John Barry
Dave Bartholomew
Fats Domino

Larry Stock
John Williams

1999
Bobby Darin
Miss Peggy Lee
Tim Rice
Bruce Springsteen

2000
James Brown
Glenn Frey (Eagles)
Don Henley (Eagles)
Curtis Mayfield
James Taylor
Brian Wilson

2001
Eric Clapton
Willie Nelson
Dolly Parton
Diane Warren
Paul Williams

2002
Nickolas Ashford
Michael Jackson
Barry Manilow
Randy Newman
Valerie Simpson
Sting

2003
Phil Collins
John Deacon
  (Queen)
Little Richard
Brian May (Queen)
Freddie Mercury
  (Queen)
Van Morrison
Roger Taylor
  (Queen)

2004
Charles Fox
Al Green
Daryl Hall
Don McLean
John Oates
Barrett Strong
Norman Whitfield

2005
David Bowie
Steve Cropper
John Fogerty
Isaac Hayes
David Porter
Richard M. Sherman
Robert B. Sherman
Bill Withers

2006
Thom Bell
Henry Cosby
Mac Davis
Will Jennings
Sylvia Moy

2007
Don Black
Irving Burgie
Jackson Browne
Merle Haggard
Michael Masser
Teddy Randazzo
Bobby Weinstein

2008
Desmond Child
Albert Hammond
Loretta Lynn
Alan Menken
John Sebastian

2009
Jon Bon Jovi
Eddie Brigati
Felix Cavaliere
Roger Cook
David Crosby
Roger Greenaway
Galt MacDermot
Graham Nash
James Rado
Gerome Ragni
Richie Sambora
Stephen Schwartz
Stephen Stills

2010
Tom Adair
Philip Bailey (Earth,
  Wind & Fire)
Leonard Cohen
Matt Dennis
Jackie DeShannon
Larry Dunn (Earth,
  Wind & Fire)
David Foster
Johnny Mandel
Bob Marley
Al McKay (Earth,
  Wind & Fire)
Laura Nyro
Sunny Skylar
Jesse Stone
Maurice White
  (Earth, Wind &
  Fire)
Verdine White
  (Earth, Wind &
  Fire)

2011
John Bettis
Garth Brooks
Tom Kelly
Leon Russell
Billy Steinberg
Allen Toussaint

2012
Tom Jones
Don Schlitz
Bob Seger
Gordon Lightfoot
Harvey Schmidt
Jim Steinman

2013
Lou Gramm
  (Foreigner)
Tony Hatch
Mick Jones
  (Foreigner)
Holly Knight
Joe Perry
  (Aerosmith)
J. D. Souther
Steven Tyler
  (Aerosmith)

2014
Ray Davies (The
  Kinks)
Donovan
Graham Gouldman
Mark James
Jim Weatherly

2015
Bobby Braddock
Willie Dixon
Jerry Garcia
Myriam Hernández
Robert Hunter
Toby Keith
Cyndi Lauper
Linda Perry

2016
Elvis Costello
Bernard Edwards
Marvin Gaye
Tom Petty
Nile Rodgers
Chip Taylor

2017
Babyface
Peter Cetera
  (Chicago)
Berry Gordy
Jimmy Jam and
  Terry Lewis

Jay-Z
Robert Lamm
  (Chicago)
Max Martin
James Pankow
  (Chicago)

2018
Bill Anderson
Robert 'Kool' Bell
  (Kool & the
  Gang)
Ronald Bell (Kool
  & the Gang)
George Brown
  (Kool & the
  Gang)
Steve Dorff
Jermaine Dupri
Alan Jackson
John Mellencamp
James 'J.T.' Taylor
  (Kool & the
  Gang)
Allee Willis

2019
Dallas Austin
Missy Elliott
Tom T. Hall
John Prine
Cat Stevens
Jack Tempchin

2020
Mariah Carey
Chad Hugo (The
  Neptunes)
Ernie Isley
Marvin Isley
O'Kelly Isley
Ronald Isley
Rudolph Isley
Chris Jasper
  (The Isley
  Brothers)
Annie Lennox
  (Eurythmics)
Steve Miller
Rick Nowels
William 'Mickey'
  Stevenson
Dave Stewart
  (Eurythmics)
Pharrell Williams
  (The Neptunes)

DOLLY WORD SEARCH

See if you can find 10 of Dolly's album and single names in the wordsearch below

(Answers on page 191)

JOLENE
TRIO
JOSHUA
WHITE LIMOZEEN
BLUE SMOKE

REAL LOVE
YELLOW ROSES
ROCKIN YEARS
HEARTBREAKER
DUMB BLONDE

W	H	I	T	E	L	I	M	O	Z	E	E	N	Y
J	J	G	P	N	L	B	C	A	D	P	D	T	E
H	U	A	L	W	Z	G	R	N	U	Q	A	W	L
E	I	Y	U	U	B	Y	E	I	M	V	C	Z	L
A	X	K	I	K	L	L	A	L	B	E	F	C	O
R	L	D	M	J	U	N	L	V	B	K	Q	G	W
T	J	J	B	Z	E	O	L	R	L	T	J	L	R
B	S	C	H	S	S	J	O	M	O	R	Q	O	O
R	O	D	B	U	M	O	V	D	N	I	L	U	S
E	T	G	U	U	O	S	E	N	D	O	M	K	E
A	W	G	S	P	K	H	O	O	E	C	S	R	S
K	E	T	S	M	E	U	J	O	L	E	N	E	U
E	B	O	P	J	A	A	F	G	I	C	U	Z	I
R	X	T	R	O	C	K	I	N	Y	E	A	R	S

DECORATE DOLLY'S DRIVE

Growing up poor, when Dolly became famous she took extra-special care of her parents. She used to buy a Cadillac for her mama and trade it in every few years for a new one. The last one she bought was a 1997 gold Cadillac. When her mama passed away, Dolly refused to get rid of it, with both she and Carl driving it for years to come.

'I call it the Dolly-Mama. Everybody knows not to mess with the Dolly-Mama because that's a precious thing!' Dolly said.

So make sure you do the Parton family proud with your new design!

★ SANDOLLAR ★ PRODUCTIONS

Dolly and her beloved former manager Sandy Gallin (1940–2017) formed the TV and movie production company Sandollar Productions in 1986. Amazingly, Dolly's involvement in the company only really became widely known in April 2020.

You may be familiar with some of their output. I know I am!

Buffy the Vampire Slayer (1997–2003)*

Angel (1999–2004)

Father of the Bride (1991)

Straight Talk (1992)

Sabrina (1995)

Father of the Bride Part II (1995)

Fly Away Home (1996)

Dolly Parton's Heartstrings (2019)

According to Sandollar executive Gail Berman, back in the 1990s, Dolly personally handed Berman a cheque when she learned that Berman received less *Buffy* royalty money than the men working at the company.

Sandollar also produced the documentary *Common Threads: Stories from the Quilt*, which won Best Documentary Feature at the 62nd Academy Awards in 1990. Narrated by Dustin Hoffman, it tells the story of the AIDS Memorial Quilt, a memorial to the people that have died of the disease and the largest piece of community folk art in history.

* Buffy's birthday is 19 January in the show, the same as Dolly's. Coincidence?

'I ALWAYS JUST THOUGHT IF YOU SEE SOMEBODY WITHOUT A SMILE, GIVE 'EM YOURS!'

FAMOUS DOLLY SONGS EMOJI QUIZ

Can you guess which one of Dolly's hits the clues are referring to?
(Answers on page 191)

1 ❤️🏹 🦋 _____

2 🧥 🌈 _____

3 ✌️ 🚪 🔽 _____

4 ☕ 🏂 _____

5 👁️ ✈️ ⛰️ _____

6 👂 🐑 🕉️ 💪 _____

WORD CLOUD — BLUE SMOKE ALBUM

Blue Smoke, inspired by the mists that shroud the Great Smoky Mountains, was Dolly's 44th solo album, released in 2014. It was Dolly's most successful album in the UK, climbing to No. 2 in the Album Chart and remaining in the Top 10 for 12 weeks.

SPOT THE DOLLY DIFFERENCE

Can you spot the seven differences between this illustration of Dolly and the one opposite? (Answers on page 191)

DOLLY BIOGRAPHY

2010–present

- Dolly appeared and performed in the 2012 musical film *Joyful Noise*, also starring Queen Latifah. The soundtrack reached No. 12 on the US Albums Chart.

- In January 2014, Dolly released the album *Blue Smoke*, which reached No. 6 on the US Pop Charts, No. 2 on both the US Country Charts and the UK Albums Chart, while it went one better in New Zealand up to No. 1. The album was later certified platinum.

- From January to July 2014, Dolly embarked on a 40-show tour to promote *Blue Smoke*, starting in Australasia, before heading to North America and Europe.

- In 2014, the Recording Industry Association of America certified Dolly's all-time worldwide sales as 100 million.

- In June 2014, Dolly played Glastonbury Festival's Pyramid Stage, performing in front of a crowd of over 180,000.

- In May 2016, Dolly and Carl renewed their vows for their 50th wedding anniversary celebration.

- In June 2016, Dolly went on a 65-date tour across Canada and the US promoting the album *Pure & Simple*, which was released in August 2016. The album was a success and saw Dolly back in her rightful place at the top of the Country Charts. It also reached No. 2 on the UK Albums Chart.

- In June 2018, Dolly earned her second star on the Hollywood

Walk of Fame with her *Trio* stars Emmylou Harris and Linda Ronstadt.

- *Heartstrings*, an eight-part series about the inspirations behind Dolly's songs, was released on Netflix in November 2019.

- Dolly recorded and released *A Holly Dolly Christmas* in October 2020, which topped the US Country Charts and reached No. 16 in the UK.

- In January 2020, Dolly Parton began what became known as the Dolly Parton Challenge, posting a four-panel image of her profile pictures on Facebook, LinkedIn, Instagram and Tinder. Inspired by her lead, millions of people around the world did the same!

- In November 2020, it was revealed that Dolly's donation of $1 million to Vanderbilt University Medical Center helped to fund the Moderna COVID-19 vaccine, which she was inoculated with on 3 March 2021. Just before the jab, she sang a parody of 'Jolene': 'Vaccine, vaccine, vaccine, vaccine, I'm begging of you please don't hesitate!'

- In February 2021, Dolly made a statement thanking the Tennessee legislature for their plans to erect a statue of her but suggested they revisit the idea later. 'Given all that's going on in the world, I don't think putting me on a pedestal is appropriate at this time,' she said.

You

Congratulations! You've won the chance to invite five people, living or dead, to a dream dinner party. We've already put Dolly at the head of the table for you, obvs. Fill in the others' names on the place-cards provided.

Dolly Parton

Dolly the Philanthropist

THE DOLLY PARTON SCHOLARSHIP

Each year, the Dollywood Foundation offers five scholarships to help Sevier County's high school seniors begin their journey into further education. The scholarship is for $15,000 and is offered to successful applicants who 'have a dream they wish to pursue and who can successfully communicate their plan and commitment to realize their dreams'.

The Foundation also offers other scholarships. In 2016, Dolly provided a $30,000 college scholarship to two-year-old Evey Johns from Conway, Arkansas, whose parents had enrolled her in Dolly's Imagination Library, her free book-gifting programme.

Dolly thought the scholarship was a fitting way to honour the library's achievement of gifting books to 1 million children each month. The money will be held in a special account and will be worth a lot more when Evey starts thinking about college!

I Beg Your Parton!

Just a quick warning that these two pages might need parents to cough loudly and flick past them quickly!

'Every now and then when I'm with my husband I'll think, "Yeah, I'll make love with Burt Reynolds tonight" — as long as it ain't Burt. My old man don't know about it, but I'm sure he wouldn't mind. I'm sure he'd make love to many people while I'm the one doin' all the work.'

INTERVIEW WITH *PEOPLE* MAGAZINE, 1982

'I've lived a lot in my time. I said I was married. I didn't say I was dead!'

INTERVIEW WITH *HOT PRESS*, 2002

'You think boobs, you think Dolly Parton.'

INTERVIEW WITH *CHICAGO TRIBUNE*, 1992

'There's only one sort of exercise I like and it ain't jogging. If I jogged, I'd end up with two black eyes.'

INTERVIEW WITH *THE TIMES*, 2011

'I make a better whore than a secretary.'

TALKING ABOUT HER ROLE IN *9 TO 5* WITH *INTERVIEW* MAGAZINE, 2012

'I can just see two big mountains growing up out of my grave, and people going on mule rides to look at them.'

ON HER FUTURE, INTERVIEW WITH REUTERS, 2007

'Some people are just born cussers. I don't even realize I'm doing it. If I have offended anybody ... tough titty.'

INTERVIEW WITH *THE TIMES*, 2011

'If I had chosen the name Dolly Dean ... I'd have been Double D. Again!'

ON CHOOSING NOT TO TAKE HER HUSBAND CARL'S NAME, INTERVIEW WITH *THE GUARDIAN*, 2014

'We hillbillies may not have sex, drugs or rock 'n' roll, but two out of three ain't bad.'

SPOKEN WHILE ACCEPTING MUSICARES PERSON OF THE YEAR AWARD, 2019

'I don't know if I'm supporting them or they're supporting me!'

INTERVIEW WITH *THE STAR*, 2018

'Are they real? They're real expensive. They're real big!'

INTERVIEW WITH *USA TODAY*, 2019

THE GREAT SMOKIES NATIONAL PARK

The park was created by the US Congress in 1934 and dedicated by President Franklin D. Roosevelt in 1940. It became a UNESCO World Heritage Site in 1983.

It's called the 'Great Smokies' because of the moisture and organic compounds given off by the dense vegetation, which is most noticeable on still summer days.

Dolly was named an ambassador for the park in 2008 to help mark the park's 75th birthday the following year.

Among the animals that live in the Smokies are 65 species of mammal, 200 types of bird, 67 native fish species, plus 80 reptile and amphibian species.

The park contains seven animal species listed as federally endangered: the Indiana bat, Carolina northern flying squirrel, Red-cockaded Woodpecker, Citico darter, Smoky madtom, Rusty-patched bumble bee and Spruce-fir moss spider.

There are over 1,500 species of flowering plants in the park.

The Great Smoky Mountains National Park, often referred to as just 'The Smokies', encompasses over 500,000 acres of land and is world-renowned for its diversity of plant and animal life. Here are some fun facts about the place that means so much to Dolly that she says,

'The Smokies are part of my DNA.'

The highest peak in the park is Clingman's Dome, at 6,643 feet. It's also the highest point in Tennessee.

The symbol and most famous resident is not in fact Dolly but the American black bear, and the national park provides the biggest protected habitat for the bears in the Eastern United States.

The National Park Service has reintroduced the river otter, elk and peregrine falcon to the Smokies, all species that had previously been driven out of the region by hunting, trapping and changing land use.

The national park has been referred to as 'the salamander capital of the world', with 30 different species in five families residing in the park.

The Smokies was the most visited national park in the US in 2019 and 2020, with 12.5 and 12.1 million visitors.

GUESS THE CELEBRITY

Can you match the quote
to the celebrity Dolly's talking about?
(Answers on page 191)

REESE WITHERSPOON

BURT REYNOLDS

WHITNEY HOUSTON

SYLVESTER STALLONE

JOHNNY CASH

ADELE

MILEY CYRUS

QUEEN LATIFAH

JENNIFER ANISTON

JANE FONDA

KENNY ROGERS

?

'She's dear to me. One of the most talented people I know, she's a great host, her comedic timing is absolutely great, she's a great actress, she sings and writes great and I just love her to pieces.'

'She asked if I would come up to her house and I was so excited to do that because I just love her to death and my husband loves her dearly so he was more excited than I was. And we went up there and she has a dog named Dolly Parton!'

?

'He's a very fine man, he's very much a father, a good husband, good friend. I love his singing, never get tired of that.'

'I've known her for years. She's a country girl too. She's a Nashville girl. She's grown up with my music. Her daddy was my ear, nose and throat doctor for years!'

?

'She plays drums, you wouldn't know that about her! When we were doing *Joyful Noise* every time there was a break, she'd get up there and start hammering on them drums, but she's great.'

'She's like a little girl to me. Working with her, there's an innocence about her but she's raw, she's rough, she's smart, she knows what she's doing.'

'I was so honoured. I was so flattered, I loved your outfit. I thought that was great. I was really touched with what you said. I was really honoured that you even know me that well or like my music, so I just wanted to thank you.' (Replying to this famous fan's tribute to her in 2018)

'I've always loved her singing, what a voice she had, at that time, nobody could out-sing her, but when I heard it, my heart just stopped. It was one of the most overwhelming things.'

'I think he's beautiful. I was surprised when I first saw him because I thought he would be gigantic ... He was more than happy to help me. I loved working with him, he's a great person.'

'I know we will always remember his funny laugh, that mischievous sparkle in his eyes, and his quirky sense of humour. You will always be my favourite sheriff, rest in peace, my little buddy, and I will always love you, Dolly.'

'He was the sexiest thing I'd ever seen. And I was looking at him, and I was feeling all those things that you feel! That's the first time I really understood what sex appeal really was.'

Positivity

'You'll never do a whole lot unless you're brave enough to try.'

'I see so much of my family in the things that I do. And I love and embrace that.'

'If your actions create a legacy that inspires others to dream more, learn more and become more, then you are an excellent leader.'

'Smile – it increases your face value!'

'When I'm inspired, I get excited because I can't wait to see what I'll come up with next.'

'The magic is inside you. There ain't no crystal ball.'

'Above everything else I've done, I've always said I've had more guts than I got talent.'

'They think I'm simple-minded because I seem so happy. Why shouldn't I be happy? I have everything I ever wanted and more. Maybe I am simple-minded. Maybe that's the key: simple.'

'Be whatever your dreams and your luck will let you.'

'What I lack in talent, I make up for in ambition and faith and determination and positive thinking.'

'I wake up every day expecting things to be good and if they're not, I set about trying to make them as good as I can. By the end of the day, I like to feel like I've tried to do my best and make that day as good a day as I can make it.'

'I don't know what the big deal is about old age. Old people who shine from the inside look 10 to 20 years younger.'

'Figure out who you are. Then do it on purpose.'

'We cannot direct the wind but we can adjust the sails.'

'I never let a rhinestone go unturned!'

Dollyopoly

I thought it'd be fun to liven up a certain board game renowned for causing tantrums (in my house anyway!) in Dolly's honour, including the places and accomplishments that are really special to her.

PARKING FREE

INCA HOOTS PRODUCTIONS

CHANCE

EAGLE MOUNTAIN SANCTUARY

GREAT SMOKY MOUNTAINS

COMMUNITY CHEST

IMAGINATION LIBRARY

DOLLYWOOD EXPRESS STEAM TRAIN

BAPTIST CHURCH, RINGGOLD, GEORGIA

GYPSY WAGON (HER GLAMOROUS TOUR BUS)

ELECTRIC COMPANY

FORMER NASHVILLE HOME

PRINTER'S ALLEY, NASHVILLE

TOOTSIE ORCHID LOU NASHVILL

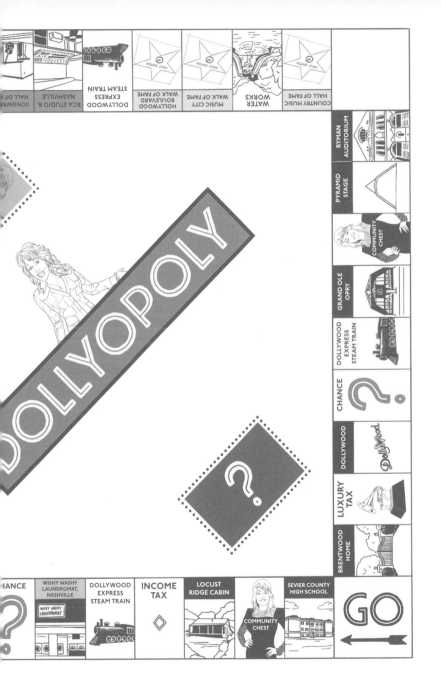

DECORATE THE SLEEVE TO DOLLY'S SECRET SONG

In Dollywood, there's a display case containing a plank of wood from Dolly's first stage and a chestnut 'dream box' that won't be opened until 19 January 2046 – the date of Dolly's 100th birthday. Inside the box is a secret song, which Dolly wrote in 2015 and recorded onto a CD. She'll need someone to design the artwork for the sleeve – over to you!

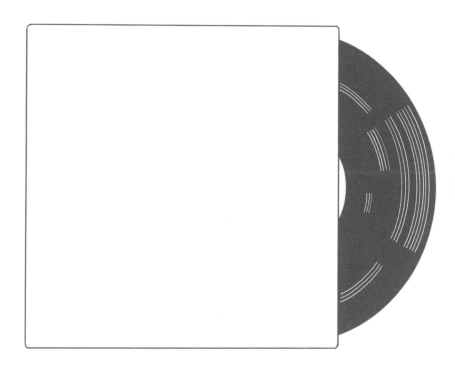

THE ULTIMATE
Dolly Parton Quiz

(Answers on page 191)

UNDER 50 CORRECT:	50–60 CORRECT:	OVER 60 CORRECT:	OVER 70 CORRECT:
Standing room	**Dress circle**	**Front of the stalls**	**VIP section!**

1 The inspiration behind the character of 'Jolene' was a real red-headed …

A Post office clerk
B Bank teller
C Waitress in a diner

2 Which state was Dolly born in?

A Tennessee
B Georgia
C Alabama

3 What is the nickname of Dolly's tour bus?

A Heartbreak Express
B Harvey the RV
C The Gypsy Wagon

4 How old was Dolly when she made her debut at the Grand Ole Opry?

A 13   **B** 16   **C** 19

5 Who famously introduced Dolly to the Grand Ole Opry stage?

A Willie Nelson
B Elvis Presley
C Johnny Cash

6 Dolly's father paid the doctor who delivered her with a sack of what?

A Flour   **B** Cornmeal   **C** Barley

7 Which city did Dolly move to the day after she graduated from high school?

A Los Angeles
B New Orleans
C Nashville

8 Dolly was the fourth of how many children?

A 6   **B** 9   **C** 12

9 What was the name of Dolly's first No. 1 single?

A Joshua   **B** Phillip   **C** David

10 Who has won the most Grammys out of Dolly, Emmylou Harris and Shania Twain?

A Dolly
B Emmylou Harris
C Shania Twain

11 Dolly was a mentor on which reality show in 2008?

A *Popstars*
B *American Idol*
C *The Voice*

12 What was the first film Dolly starred in?

A *9 to 5*
B *The Best Little Whorehouse in Texas*
C *Steel Magnolias*

13 Dolly provided a race announcer's voice in which 2011 3D animated film?

A *Gnomeo & Juliet*
B *Happy Feet Two*
C *Puss in Boots*

14 Dolly has a cameo in which 2005 film sequel?

A *Cheaper by the Dozen 2*
B *Batman Begins*
C *Miss Congeniality 2*

15 Which of the cast of *Steel Magnolias* won a Golden Globe for Best Supporting Actress?

A Dolly Parton
B Julia Roberts
C Sally Field

16 In 1999, Dolly lent her voice to an episode of which animated TV series?

A *Family Guy*
B *The Simpsons*
C *South Park*

17 Over the course of her career, Dolly has composed approximately how many songs?

A 1,000　　B 3,000　　C 5,000

18 In which year did Whitney Houston cover 'I Will Always Love You' for the soundtrack to *The Bodyguard*?

A 1999　　B 1992　　C 1994

19 Who did Dolly reject in 1974 after their manager insisted on a 50/50 split of publishing rights?

A Frank Sinatra
B Johnny Cash
C Elvis Presley

20 Who was Dolly's co-star in *The Best Little Whorehouse in Texas*?

A Burt Reynolds
B Sylvester Stallone
C Tom Selleck

21 Dolly first won Entertainer of the Year at the Grammys in the year that *Star Wars* was released – which year was it?

A 1975　　B 1976　　C 1977

22 At the 53rd Academy Awards in 1982, Dolly's '9 to 5' lost out on the award of Best Original Song to which song?

A 'Fame'
B 'On the Road Again'
C 'Endless Love'

23 Who was Dolly's duet partner for the 1983 hit 'Islands in the Stream'?

A Barry Gibb
B Kenny Rogers
C Kris Kristofferson

24 Dolly Parton is godmother to which pop star?

A Britney Spears
B Taylor Swift
C Miley Cyrus

25 What was Dolly's only solo No. 1 on the US Billboard 100 Chart?

A 'Jolene'
B '9 to 5'
C 'I Will Always Love You'

26 Dolly accepted a regular spot on which syndicated TV programme in 1967?

A *The Porter Wagoner Show*
B *The Tonight Show Starring Johnny Carson*
C *The Ed Sullivan Show*

27 In 2018, Dolly admitted on *The Tonight Show Starring Jimmy Fallon* that her husband had fantasies about which actor?

A Courteney Cox
B Lisa Kudrow
C Jennifer Aniston

28 Spot the made-up Dolly song title:

A 'Heartbreaker'
B 'Heartbreak High'
C 'Heartbreak Express'

29 Dolly's *Trio* involved Dolly and which two stars?

A Emmylou Harris and Linda Ronstadt
B Loretta Lynn and Linda Ronstadt
C Emmylou Harris and Tammy Wynette

30 In 2019, Dolly celebrated how many years as a member of the Grand Ole Opry?

A 30　　　　B 40　　　　C 50

31 In 2016, Dolly celebrated which wedding anniversary with her husband Carl?

A 40th　　　B 50th　　　C 60th

32 Dolly came up with the iconic typewriter clacking rhythm in the song '9 to 5' by doing what on the set of the movie?

A Tapping her acrylic nails
B Grinding her teeth
C Tapping two hairclips

33 Which year was the film and song '9 to 5' released?

A 1980   **B** 1982   **C** 1984

34 Which of the Democratic contenders for the 2020 Presidential nomination frequently played '9 to 5' in campaign appearances?

A Elizabeth Warren
B Bernie Sanders
C Amy Klobuchar

35 What was Dollywood known as before Dolly became the co-owner?

A Golden Nugget City
B Silver Dollar City
C Barnstormer

36 Which year did Dolly become co-owner of the park that would become known as Dollywood?

A 1982   **B** 1984   **C** 1986

37 The Dollywood logo famously features which creature?

A A bird   **B** A butterfly   **C** A bear

38 What is the name of the National Park in Tennessee that Dolly has become closely associated with?

A Rocky Mountain
B Great Smoky Mountains
C Shenandoah

39 Who was Dolly's co-star in the 1984 film *Rhinestone*?

A Sylvester Stallone
B Christopher Walken
C Kris Kristofferson

40 Who is the only woman to have scored more Grammy nominations than Dolly?

A Whitney Houston
B Beyoncé
C Lauryn Hill

41 Dolly and Carl first met outside which business?

A Laundromat
B Post office
C Bank

42 'Rockin' Years' was a 1991 hit duet with which musician?

A Waylon Jennings
B John Denver
C Ricky Van Shelton

43 Who is the only woman to appear above Dolly on *Rolling Stone*'s 100 Greatest Country Artists of all Time in 2017?

A Loretta Lynn
B Shania Twain
C June Carter Cash

44 The Music City Walk of Fame is located in which US city?

A Los Angeles **B** Chicago   **C** Nashville

45 Dolly's first hit country single was called what?

A 'Blonde Joke'
B 'Dumb Blonde'
C 'Stupid Blonde'

46 Dolly played Glastonbury for the first time in which year?

A 2014   **B** 2016   **C** 2018

47 Which song does Dolly traditionally end her concerts with?

A 'Jolene'
B 'Islands in the Stream'
C 'I Will Always Love You'

48 Which stage did Dolly play when she headlined Glastonbury?

A Park   **B** Pyramid   **C** John Peel

49 Dolly made a surprise appearance at the Newport Folk Festival, in which diminutive US state?

A Rhode Island
B Delaware
C Connecticut

50 The Grammys are now held in the Staples Center in which US city?

A New York
B Miami
C Los Angeles

51 As of March 2021, how many solo studio albums has Dolly made?

A 27   **B** 37   **C** 47

52 Which musician, born Alecia Beth Moore, sang 'Jolene' at Dolly's MusiCares award tribute concert in 2019?

A Pink   **B** Beyoncé   **C** Cher

53 Don Henley sang Dolly's 1991 hit 'Eagle When She Flies' at Dolly's MusiCares tribute concert in 2019, but which band was Henley associated with?

A Fleetwood Mac
B Eagles
C Aerosmith

54 Dolly appeared on the October 1978 cover of which magazine wearing a Playboy Bunny outfit?

A *The Face*
B *Playboy*
C *Rolling Stone*

55 What was the name of Dolly's 2019 Netflix series?

A *Coat-tails*
B *Heartstrings*
C *Love handles*

56 Which one of Dolly's siblings reached the Country Top 10 in 1975 with 'I Want to Hold You in My Dreams Tonight'?

A Rachel   **B** Stella   **C** Randy

57 Which of the following has Dolly not been inducted into?

A Country Music Hall of Fame
B Gospel Hall of Fame
C Blues Hall of Fame

58 Which COVID-19 vaccine did Dolly's generous $1 million donation go towards?

A Moderna
B Pfizer
C AstraZeneca

59 Which late-night show host did Dolly move to tears in October 2020 when she broke into a song that her mother used to sing her?

A Stephen Colbert
B Jimmy Fallon
C Jimmy Kimmel

60 Which US city does Dolly live on the outskirts of?

A Los Angeles
B Nashville
C Miami

61 Dolly's two weaknesses, by her own admission, are what and what?

A 'Lipstick and eyeliner'
B 'Nip and tucks'
C 'Food and men'

62 Dolly's fragrance, launched in July 2021 is called …

A Scent from Above
B Parton Parfum
C Eau Dolly!

63 In 2012, Dolly admitted to having a crush on which singer?

A Kris Kristofferson
B Johnny Cash
C Kenny Rogers

64 Which artist painted Dolly in 1985?

A David Hockney
B Roy Lichtenstein
C Andy Warhol

65 Dolly was interviewed in her home by which Hollywood A-list actor in the first episode of a 2018 talk show series?

A Reese Witherspoon
B Nicole Kidman
C Gwyneth Paltrow

66 Which fellow music superstar posted an Instagram tribute in January 2018 dressed up as Dolly with the caption: 'The effortless queen of song, Dolly Parton!'?

A Katy Perry
B Adele
C Beyoncé

67 What is the name of Dolly's book-gifting programme?

A Imagination Library
B Rainbow Library
C Unicorn Library

68 Dolly was the name of the most famous cloned animal, but what type of animal was she?

A Dog   **B** Sheep   **C** Cat

69 What was Dolly's first pop crossover hit, reaching No. 1 in the Country Charts and No. 3 on the Billboard Hot 100 in 2017?

A 'Here I Go Again'
B 'There You Go Again'
C 'Here You Come Again'

70 Dolly's Pure & Simple tour was her last major international tour but which year was it?

A 2016   **B** 2018   **C** 2020

71 '9 to 5 The Musical' hit Broadway in 2009 but which actor, who won a Best Supporting Actress Oscar in 2017, played office supervisor Violet Newstead?

A Laura Dern
B Allison Janney
C Maggie Gyllenhaal

72 Sylvester Stallone turned down the lead role in which film of 1984, directed by Robert Zemeckis, to star in *Rhinestone* alongside Dolly?

A *Romancing the Stone*
B *Back to the Future*
C *Who Framed Roger Rabbit*

73 In 1982, Dolly lost out to which English actor for the Golden Globe for Best Actress in Comedy or Musical?

A Judi Dench
B Maggie Smith
C Julie Andrews

74 What was Dolly's character's name in *The Best Little Whorehouse in Texas*?

A Rhona Tangley
B Mona Stangley
C Fiona Hangley

75 What was Dolly's character's name in *9 to 5*?

A Doralee Rhodes
B Peggy Sue Rhodes
C Dotty Mae Rhodes

76 '9 to 5' knocked which song by Kool & the Gang off the top of the Billboard Hot 100 in 1980?

A 'Locomotion'
B 'Imagination'
C 'Celebration'

77 Dolly's duet 'Islands in the Stream' knocked which song by Bonnie Tyler off the top of the Billboard Hot 100 in 1983?

A 'Total Eclipse of the Heart'
B 'Partial Eclipse of the Heart'
C 'Solar Eclipse in my Heart'

78 Which Lionel Richie song knocked 'Islands in the Stream' off the top of the Billboard Hot 100 in 1983?

A 'All Day Long'
B 'All Night Long'
C 'All Weekend Long'

79 Which No. 1 single on the Billboard Hot 100 of 1983 held the top spot for the most weeks?

A 'Islands in the Stream'
B 'Billie Jean'
C 'Every Breath You Take'

80 '9 to 5' was the third-highest grossing film of 1981 in the US, but what was the first?

A *Raiders of the Lost Ark*
B *The Blues Brothers*
C *Airplane!*

81 Which actor, Pulitzer- winning playwright and director plays Dolly's husband in *Steel Magnolias*?

A Arthur Miller
B Sam Shepard
C Tom Stoppard

82 Which of Dolly's co-stars in *Steel Magnolias* won the Best Actress Academy award for her performance in *Terms of Endearment*?

A Sally Field
B Shirley MacLaine
C Daryl Hannah

83 Dolly's third bluegrass-inspired album, *Halos & Horns*, included a cover of which rock classic?

A 'Stairway to Heaven' by Led Zeppelin
B 'Layla' by Derek and the Dominos
C 'Start Me Up' by The Rolling Stones

84 Who did Dolly present the award for Best Pop Vocal Performance, Female, to at the 1994 Grammy Awards?

A Mariah Carey
B Tina Turner
C Whitney Houston

85 Who presented Dolly with the Hitmaker Award at the Billboard Women in Music event in 2020?

A Ariana Grande
B Miley Cyrus
C Rihanna

86 In 2014, Dolly put three of her properties on the market in which US state?

A Hawaii
B California
C Utah

87 Dolly's classic album of 1980, *9 to 5 and Odd Jobs*, included a version of which traditional folk song also famously recorded by The Animals in 1964?

A 'Oh Shenandoah'
B 'The House of the Rising Sun'
C 'Keep on the Sunny Side'

88 Dolly won the Grammy's Lifetime Achievement Award in which year?

A 2001   **B** 2006   **C** 2011

89 In February 2021, Dolly announced that she didn't want a statue of her, saying, 'Given all that's going on in the world, I don't think putting me on a pedestal is appropriate at this time.' Where was the statue going to be erected?

A Lincoln Park, Washington DC
B Tennessee State Capitol
C Central Park, New York

TRUE OR FALSE?

90 'Jolene' is the only one of Dolly's songs to make *Rolling Stone*'s 500 Greatest Songs of All Time in 2004.

91 Dolly has been awarded two honorary doctorates.

92 Carl has never seen Dolly perform.

93 Dolly once went on a date with Kermit the Frog.

94 Dolly was born Dorothy Avie Lee Parton.

95 The idea for the film *9 to 5* was Dolly's.

96 Dolly has never had a single reach No. 1 in the UK.

97 As of March 2021, Dolly has never appeared on *RuPaul's Drag Race*.

98 Jennifer Aniston has a dog named Dolly Parton.

99 Dolly rejected the lead role in the film *Splash*.

100 Dolly's first Grammy Award win was in 1976.

ANSWER PAGES

PAGES 8–9: DOLLY TRUE OR FALSE?

Here are the four lies hiding among the extraordinary truths!

- Dolly was originally cast to play Sugar 'Kane' Kowalczyk in *Some Like It Hot* before the role went to Marilyn Monroe
- The British confectionery 'Dolly mixture' is named after Dolly
- Dolly was made an honorary Dame by Queen Elizabeth II in 2001
- Dolly tried to buy Disneyland Paris in 1993 after a disappointing opening year for the park

PAGE 25: WHERE'S DOLLY?

Answer to come answer to come answer to come answer to come.

PAGE 29: 1946 QUIZ

1. Freddie Mercury
2. George W. Bush
3. Sylvester Stallone
4. Cher
5. Alan Rickman
6. Steven Spielberg
7. Al Green
8. Liza Minnelli
9. Gianni Versace
10. Susan Sarandon

PAGE 31: SONG ANAGRAMS

1. Jolene
2. I Will Always Love You
3. Islands in the Stream
4. Love Is Like a Butterfly
5. Apple Jack
6. Yellow Roses
7. Coat of Many Colors
8. Heartbreaker
9. Wildflowers
10. Nine to Five (I know it's '9 to 5' but that would have been a really easy anagram!)

PAGES 34–35: SPOT THE DOLLY DIFFERENCE

1. Apple replaced with book
2. Book missing on shelf above the apple
3. Light is switched on/off
4. Missing book on pile fifth shelf from bottom
5. Framed picture of star/rainbow
6. Pattern/no pattern on flower pot
7. Shapes rearranged on spine of book on top shelf

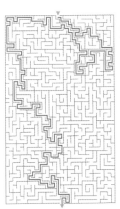

PAGE 36: 'FIND THE GUITAR' MAZE

PAGES 42–43: FAMOUS TENNESSEANS QUIZ

1. Morgan Freeman
2. Quentin Tarantino
3. Tina Turner
4. Kathy Bates
5. Aretha Franklin
6. Justin Timberlake
7. Davy Crockett
8. Johnny Knoxville
9. Miley Cyrus
10. Isaac Hayes
11. Jack Daniel
12. Reese Witherspoon
13. Nicole Kidman
14. Taylor Swift
15. Kelly Clarkson

PAGE 44: DOLLY WORDSEARCH

```
J  B  V  S  I  Q  C  E  K  L  A  I  X  I
E  U  R  N  A  S  H  V  I  L  L  E  O  J
H  T  Y  X  Z  P  A  C  U  B  L  G  V  K
E  T  S  Z  S  M  O  K  I  E  S  F  E  T
A  E  F  X  A  I  R  R  O  P  R  Y  E  E
R  R  Q  Y  R  D  Y  K  T  P  Y  K  X  N
T  F  S  U  Z  C  O  N  B  E  G  V  Y  N
S  L  P  R  E  G  C  L  Y  Y  R  S  C  E
T  Y  Z  K  V  K  O  S  L  V  F  T  H  S
R  J  Y  B  A  H  U  S  C  Y  B  J  I  S
I  U  X  F  C  Z  N  G  A  Z  W  I  U  E
N  N  W  U  F  U  T  V  R  H  X  O  L  E
G  I  Z  J  H  J  R  J  L  L  V  P  O  Y
S  O  S  L  W  L  Y  L  A  Q  C  Q  X  D
```

PAGE 53: WHERE'S DOLLY?

On the spine of a book sitting on the middle of the second shelf.

PAGE 58: SIX DEGREES OF KEVIN BACON

DOLLY PARTON > JULIA ROBERTS (*Steel Magnolias*) > MATT DAMON (*Mystic Pizza*)

DOLLY PARTON > SYLVESTER STALLONE (*Rhinestone*) > ARNOLD SCHWARZENEGGER (*The Expendables 2*)

DOLLY PARTON > SANDRA BULLOCK (*Miss Congeniality 2*) > KEANU REEVES (*Speed*)

DOLLY PARTON > SALLY FIELD (*Steel Magnolias*) > EMMA STONE (*The Amazing Spider-Man*) > OLIVIA COLMAN (*The Favourite*)

DOLLY PARTON > JANE FONDA (*9 to 5*) > JENNIFER LOPEZ (*Monster-in-Law*) > STANLEY TUCCI (*Maid in Manhattan*) > MERYL STREEP (*The Devil Wears Prada/Julie & Julia*)

PAGE 60: KENNEDY CENTER HONOREES QUIZ: ACTORS

1. Tom Hanks (*Apollo 13*)
2. James Earl Jones (*The Empire Strikes Back*)
3. Charlton Heston (*Planet of the Apes*)
4. Sean Connery (*Goldfinger*)
5. Robert De Niro (*Taxi Driver*)
6. Julie Andrews (*Mary Poppins*)
7. Meryl Streep (*The Devil Wears Prada*)
8. Al Pacino (*The Godfather Part II*)
9. Morgan Freeman (*The Shawshank Redemption*)
10. Sally Field (*Forrest Gump*)

PAGE 61: KENNEDY CENTER HONOREES QUIZ: SINGERS

1. Paul McCartney ('Yesterday')
2. Tina Turner ('What's Love Got to Do with It')
3. Neil Diamond ('Sweet Caroline')
4. Chuck Berry ('You Never Can Tell')
5. Cher ('Believe')
6. Paul Simon ('You Can Call Me Al')
7. Diana Ross ('Upside Down')
8. Johnny Cash ('Folsom Prison Blues')
9. James Brown ('I Got You (I Feel Good)')
10. Aretha Franklin ('Respect')

PAGE 72: WHERE'S DOLLY?

Hiding behind a tree on the right hand side.

PAGE 82: DOLLY DOES TWITTER

1. Reese Witherspoon (Reese's with-a-spoon)
2. Foo Fighters (Food Fighters)
3. Oprah Winfrey (Opera Win-free)
4. Macy Gray (Macy's Grey)
5. Jane Fonda (Jane Fonder)
6. Tyra Banks (Tyre Banks)
7. Perez Hilton (Pére-Z- Hilton)
8. Katy Perry (K-tee Perry)
9. Kenny Rogers (Ken-Knee Rogers)
10. Jimmy Fallon (Jimmy Fall-on)

PAGE 85: DOLLY CROSSWORD

ACROSS	DOWN
4. Pyramid	1. Playboy
6. Memphis	2. Cyrus
9. Heartstrings	3. Fiftieth
11. Randy	5. Aquarius
12. Bluegrass	7. Moderna
13. Reese	8. Bald eagle
	10. Tomlin
	12. Black

PAGE 86: DOLLY'S BIRTHDAY QUIZ

1. Paul Cézanne
2. Stefan Edberg
3. Phil Everly

4. Edgar Allan Poe
5. James Watt
6. Janis Joplin
7. Jenson Button
8. Martin Bashir
9. Pete Buttigieg
10. Patricia Highsmith

PAGES 90–91: SPOT THE DOLLY DIFFERENCE

1. Changed colour on bottom chariot on left Ferris wheel
2. Ticket booth open sign
3. Central star missing on pirate ship
4. Central star/circle motif on right Ferris wheel
5. Cloud above right Ferris wheel appeared
6. Missing star on top of the chair swing
7. Pattern on balloon reversed

PAGE 92: WOODROW WILSON AWARD WINNERS

ROLE	NAME
President of Brazil (2011–2016)	Dilma Rousseff
Architect behind the Guggenheim Museum in Bilbao	Frank Gehry
US Secretary of State (2001–2005)	Colin Powell
Commander of US Central Command (2008–2010)	David Petraeus
Legendary composer of musicals	Andrew Lloyd Webber
Multiple Grammy-award-winning superstar	Dolly Parton
Prime Minister of Australia (1996–2007)	John Howard
First Lady of the USA (1974–1977)	Betty Ford
Male golfer with the most major championship wins	Jack Nicklaus
Long-serving Arizona senator and former navy officer	John McCain
First woman nominated by a major political party for President	Hillary Clinton

PAGE 106: EGOT QUIZ

1. Audrey Hepburn
2. Rita Moreno

3. John Gielgud
4. Mel Brooks
5. Whoopi Goldberg
6. John Legend
7. Barbra Streisand
8. Liza Minnelli
9. James Earl Jones
10. Andrew Lloyd Webber

PAGE 107: WHERE'S DOLLY?

Hidden among the foliage on the left-hand side of the image.

PAGE 108: WALK OF FAME QUIZ

1. Bob Hope
2. Ringo Starr
3. Dean Martin
4. George Harrison
5. Frank Sinatra
6. Diana Ross
7. John Lennon
8. Smokey Robinson
9. Michael Jackson
10. Bing Crosby

PAGE 115: DOLLY BOGGLE

Here are (almost all) the words that you can make from the boggle board. I've left out some that no one's ever heard of/you need a dictionary to prove because that's no fun! It's one point for the words with 4 or fewer letters and 2 points for words of five letters and above.

Throttle	Throe	Then
Troutlet	Totty	Thou
Bettor	Troth	Tone
Outfly	Trout	Tort
Outlet	Tufty	Tote
Rotten	Belt	Tour
Throne	Bene	Tout
Bento	Bent	Trot
Futon	Hone	Tuft
Honey	Hour	Turf
Hotel	Into	Bel
Hotly	Lent	Bet
Intro	Note	Bin
North	Rote	Elf
Tenor	Rout	Fly
Thein	Tent	Fur

Hen	Not	Tie
Hoe	One	Toe
Hon	Our	Ton
Hot	Out	Tor
Let	Roe	Tot
Ley	Rot	Tye
Net	Rut	Yen
Nib	Ten	Yet
Nor	The	

PAGE 118: GLASTONBURY HEADLINERS QUIZ

1. Pulp
2. Beyoncé
3. Stormzy
4. Kings of Leon
5. Jay-Z
6. Blur
7. Foo Fighters
8. Kylie Minogue
9. Adele
10. Bruce Springsteen

PAGE 122: DOLLY CROSSWORD

ACROSS	DOWN
1. Butterfly	1. Bush
4. Joshua	2. Georgia
5. Twelve	3. Dean
7. Ten	5. Tennessee
8. Nashville	6. Dollywood
10. Rhinestone	9. Reynolds
11. Harris	10 Rebecca

PAGE 132: DOLLY BOGGLE

As above, here are (almost all) the words that you can make from the boggle board.

It's one point for the words with 4 or fewer letters and 2 points for words of five letters and above.

Raincoats	Atonic	Atone
Raincoat	Canopy	Canal
Arnicas	Dollar	Coast
Asocial	Enrapt	Coats
Polaric	Plaice	Costa
Apneic	Social	Lance
Anica	Stance	Nasty
Atonal	Alloy	Panic

Plain	Nice	Can
Plane	Nota	Cat
Soapy	Oast	Con
Sonar	Oats	Cop
Sonic	Once	Cos
Stone	Opal	Cot
Tacos	Opts	Coy
Tonal	Pain	Ice
Tonic	Pair	Lap
Typos	Pall	Lop
Acne	Pane	Nap
Atop	Plan	Not
Cane	Plod	Oar
Cast	Ploy	Oat
Cats	Poll	One
Ciao	Post	Opt
Cine	Pots	Pal
Coal	Rain	Pan
Coat	Rapt	Pod
Cone	Rice	Pot
Copt	Sane	Ran
Copy	Soap	Rap
Cost	Soar	Sat
Cots	Stop	Son
Doll	Taco	Soy
Icon	Tone	Sty
Inca	Typo	Tan
Lain	Ace	Ton
Lair	Air	Top
Lane	All	Toy
Loan	Apt	

PAGE 135: WHERE'S DOLLY?

Featured on a guitar label on the top rack of guitars.

PAGE 138–139: SPOT THE DOLLY DIFFERENCE

1. Fallen leaves on rock
2. Tortoise
3. Missing tree trunk in centre of frame
4. Snake
5. Fox awake/sleeping
6. Boar
7. Lizard

PAGE 146: WHERE'S DOLLY?

In the crowd on the left-hand side of the image.

PAGE 153: NATIONAL MEDAL OF ARTS WINNERS

1. Arthur Miller
2. Ray Charles
3. Maya Angelou
4. Bob Dylan
5. Harper Lee
6. Al Pacino
7. Morgan Freeman
8. George Lucas
9. Barbra Streisand
10. Angela Lansbury

PAGE 158: DOLLY WORDSEARCH

PAGE 162: FAMOUS DOLLY SONGS EMOJI QUIZ

1. *Love Is Like a Butterfly*
2. *Coat of Many Colors*
3. *Two Doors Down*
4. *Jolene* (cup of Joe, leaning)
5. *Islands in the Stream* (eye, lands, stream)
6. *Here You Come Again* (hear, ewe, karma, gain)

PAGES 164–165: SPOT THE DOLLY DIFFERENCE

1. Missing label on guitar on top rack
2. Picture frames on the wall swapped
3. Logo on amplifier missing
4. Sound hole on guitar on top rack missing
5. Different colour of bridge on guitar on bottom rack
6. Guitar colour change on top rack
7. Star missing on amplifier

PAGE 174: GUESS THE CELEBRITY

'She's dear to me …' (Miley Cyrus)
'She asked if I would come up to her house …' (Jennifer Aniston)
'I've known her for years …' (Reese Witherspoon)
'I was so honoured …' (Adele)
'I've always loved her singing …' (Whitney Houston)
'He's a very fine man …' (Kenny Rogers)
'She's like a little girl to me …' (Jane Fonda)
'She plays drums …' (Queen Latifah)
'I know we will always remember his funny laugh …' (Burt Reynolds)
'I think he's beautiful …' (Sylvester Stallone)
'He was the sexiest thing I'd ever seen …' (Johnny Cash)

PAGES 181–186: THE ULTIMATE DOLLY PARTON QUIZ

1. B	19. C	37. B	55. B	73. C
2. A	20. A	38. B	56. B	74. B
3. C	21. C	39. A	57. C	75. A
4. C	22. A	40. B	58. A	76. C
5. C	23. B	41. A	59. A	77. A
6. B	24. C	42. C	60. B	78. B
7. C	25. B	43. A	61. C	79. C
8. C	26. A	44. C	62. A	80. A
9. A	27. C	45. B	63. B	81. B
10. B	28. B	46. A	64. C	82. B
11. B	29. A	47. C	65. A	83. A
12. A	30. C	48. B	66. B	84. C
13. A	31. B	49. A	67. A	85. B
14. C	32. A	50. C	68. B	86. C
15. B	33. A	51. C	69. C	87. B
16. B	34. A	52. A	70. A	88. C
17. B	35. B	53. B	71. B	89. C
18. B	36. C	54. B	72. A	

90. TRUE
91. TRUE
92. FALSE (he has seen her only once!)
93. TRUE!
94. FALSE
95. FALSE (it was Jane Fonda's idea)
96. TRUE
97. TRUE
98. TRUE
99. FALSE
100. FALSE

ACKNOWLEDGEMENTS

Enormous thanks to my wife, best friend, office-mate, sounding board, quality controller and all-round superstar **Tarah Coonan-Joyce**. And to our wonderful little boy **Finn**, who makes us giggle more and more every day with his bouncy dance moves. And to the irrepressible **Paul Joyce**, in the year of his long-awaited retrospective exhibition!

A big thank you to my agent and all round fine fellow **Ben Dunn**.

Thanks to **John Reeder** both for introducing me to the incredible trio and for kindly sending me Dolly's first foray into bluegrass (on a CD no less).

To **Izzy Holton**, **Alice Kennedy-Owen**, **Ian Allen** and **Phil Brown** for your hard work, and to **Sally Bond** for making this book look terrific. And **Juhee Kim**, your fantastic illustrations really light the book up.

And good golly, Miss **Dolly** (I really wanted to say that somewhere in the book), you make everyone's lives that little bit better. I'll be in the front row when you next grace our shores. Please let it be Brighton Pride 2022!

Finally, a huge thank you to all of you lovely folks who have bought these books, which have been so much fun to put together!